Superhero Educator

Superhero Educator

HOW TO TEACH WITH SUPERIOR SKILLS AND SUCCESS

Dr. Steve Gerner & Eugene Pitchford III

ISBN-13: 9781979574945
ISBN-10: 1979574944

Preface

These staggering statistics highlight a great need.

- The United States ranks 27th out of 64 countries in math.
- The United States ranks 20th out of 64 countries in science.
- The United States spends more money per student than any other country (Digest of Education Statistics, 2015).
- Only 40% of 4th graders are proficient in math.
- Only 36% of 4th graders are proficient in science.
- 6.4 million children between the ages of four and seventeen have been diagnosed with Attention Deficit Hyperactivity Disorder (ADHD).
- The achievement gap between black and white students in math is 30% (Desilver, 2017).

In addition to all these challenges, teachers are struggling with classroom management, meeting of diverse learners, and desperately trying to learn how to utilize data to improve instruction.

Gotham City is burning!

We need help! We need a superhero. We need many superheroes. An army of superheroes is necessary to battle low expectations, crushing poverty, lack of student engagement, and student apathy, even despair. Reviewing these statistics may leave anyone feeling hopeless and even depressed. However, the great news is that outstanding educators break through the chaos to transform students' lives. We call these brilliant performers **SUPERHERO EDUCATORS**.

Acknowledgements

Dr. Steve Gerner

I thank my parents for their lives of steadfast service to others, for instilling in me the strong work ethic they both embody, and their commitment to raise me with an abiding faith in Jesus Christ.

I thank my loving and gracious wife for her never-ending patience, her enduring support, and her solid commitment to lifelong learning.

I thank our three precious children for the joy they bring daily to our family with their unique personalities, incredible humor, and enriching conversations.

Thank you to the numerous students that I have been blessed to reach and teach throughout my career for growing with me, educating me, and shaping me into a **SUPERHERO EDUCATOR**.

Finally I thank EP3. Your flexibility, your ability to think big, and your friendship is always valued.

Eugene Pitchford

I thank my wife for her unwavering support. Thank you for giving me the thumbs up on this project. You are a **SUPERHERO EDUCATOR** and Wife.

I thank our three children. Hopefully I am inspiring you to be great! Continue to dream with your eyes open.

I thank my Mom, Aunt Gloria, and Grandmother for always pushing me past my comfort zone. You are all my real life Superheroes.

Thank you to all of the **SUPERHERO EDUCATORS** I have worked with in my career. There are too many to name. I appreciate you and will forever honor you.

Finally, to Notorious G. – Thank you and dream BIG!

A special thank you to <u>Autumn Harrington</u> and <u>Taylor Rystrom</u> for creating informative illustrations. Autumn and Taylor are true professionals.

About the Authors

Dr. Steve Gerner is a professor, educational strategist, author, and driven leader passionate about developing high-performing educators that directly impact all students' success. Relentlessly driven to improve student performance, much of his work centers on teacher quality, city education, and classroom management. Dr. Gerner started his career as an elementary school teacher and principal. He still influences the field of education as well as the business community through powerful presentations and relevant teaching. Currently, Dr. Gerner is Dean of Students and Professor of Education at Concordia University Wisconsin.

Professor Eugene Pitchford III is a professor, scholar, leader, author, husband, father, and the #1 sports fan in America. He is passionate about helping educators become equipped to meet the challenging demands of being successful in a school environment. Eugene often speaks on urban education issues as well as motivational speaking for schools, community organizations, and parent groups. Currently, Eugene Pitchford is Professor of Education and Faculty Advisor to the Black Student Union at Concordia University Wisconsin.

Email: superheroeducator@gmail.com
Continue the Conversation on Facebook – Search: **Superhero Educator**
Twitter: @superheroedu

Format of the Book

SUPERHERO EDUCATOR: *How to Teach with Superior Skills and Success* is an indispensable handbook for all educators. New and future educators will find the information valuable as they shape their teaching philosophy and develop their delivery skills. Experienced teachers will be able to refine their teaching talents and learn novel ways to grow professionally. Any individual who influences others through education, instruction, and training will greatly benefit from this book.

Each chapter consists of the following components:

Superhero Connection
This paragraph reflects on the strengths of a variety of superheroes and the links they provide to educator themes.

Impact Story
These pages set the stage for the chapter by highlighting and exhibiting the importance of each educator theme.

Innovative Connections
Innovation is essential for 21st century schools. The distinct chapter themes successfully mesh with these creative connections. In many instances, direct

transfers will be made from these concepts to our professional educational settings.

Educational Research and Focus

Current educational research makes these sections extremely relevant. As the nucleus of the book, this portion provides the context to assist teachers in their evaluation of a variety of educational scenarios.

Diagram

The diagrams toward the end of each chapter provide a visual reinforcement for the reader. These memorable visuals supply a deeper application of the theme.

Debriefing Questions

These vital questions allow you, the reader, to reflect on your professional walk. Answering these questions will cause you to become a stronger and better-equipped professional.

Notes of Emphasis

Each chapter ends with a place for writing notes and for making comments that come to mind as you read. Regardless of whether your notes are natural connections or powerful applications, your written thoughts will foster a wiser scholar. Please, take as many notes as you like and reference them often.

Let this book be your guide as you continue on the path towards **SUPERHERO EDUCATOR** status.

Names and identifying details of people and schools have been changed to protect the privacy of individuals.

Table of Contents

Introduction

Who is your favorite superhero? As a young child I dreamed of leaping off a building like Batman, scaling a building like Spiderman, commanding the waterworld like Aquaman, or battling evil villains with powerful rings like Green Lantern. Recently, superheroes like Catwoman, Captain America, Blade, Black Panther, and Iron Man have captured our imaginations. Superheroes possess supernatural powers that are put into action to protect the public. Superheroes wear costumes to protect their identity and to assist in fighting evil. Superheroes give us hope and allow us a chance to imagine a better world. From the very young to the young at heart, we can all imagine ourselves as superheroes. We picture what it is like to destroy evil and save the world. Even when the outcome looks bleak, superheroes find a pathway to victory. Success is achieved through the use of their talents and superior skills.

High-performing educators easily equate to superheroes. Since educators have the power to transform lives and provide tremendous hope, the superhero analogy is well-suited. With superior skills and success, **SUPERHERO EDUCATORS** make the world a better place. To gain **SUPERHERO EDUCATOR** status, novel training and learning must occur. We evaluated educators in both urban and non-urban environments over the past two decades, and identifiable qualities for successful teaching surfaced repeatedly. After countless conversations and observations, contemplating what characterizes great teachers, we coined the term **SUPERHERO EDUCATORS**. Every successful teacher has special "powers" and puts those powers into practice on a daily basis.

This book provides the blueprint for teachers to become true **SUPERHERO EDUCATORS**. Whether it is constructing a workable relationship to foster new understanding or relating the theories of Nikola Tesla in simple terms to your students, we need superheroes. We believe **SUPERHERO EDUCATORS** excel in the upcoming identified criteria. While reading this book you have the opportunity to reflect on your strengths and weaknesses. Where there are areas that need improvement, this book will be your roadmap for success. Where there are areas of strengths, this book will help you maximize outcomes. A **SUPERHERO EDUCATOR** is a teacher who possesses outstanding talents and is dedicated to fighting low student expectations, protecting all students, and battling against unproductive learning environments.

CHAPTER 1
A Calling

Superhero Connection

We all love the Incredible Hulk for his brute strength and aggressiveness. His power is beyond the strength of any human. When the Incredible Hulk becomes upset due to an injustice, his body turns green. The transition from being normal to becoming a green muscle machine is what makes the Incredible Hulk different from all other superheroes. **SUPERHERO EDUCATORS** *clearly understand their mission and calling, which is more than a job. Like the Incredible Hulk, they are "all in" with great passion, vigorous energy, and limitless knowledge.*

Impact Story

Why do you teach? The answer to this question defines your calling, your mission for being a teacher.

Facebook CEO Mark Zuckerberg is on a mission to give away 99% of his Facebook shares during his lifetime. This offering is valued at over 45 billion dollars (Carson, 2015). In fact, several of the world's wealthiest individuals have announced their intention to join Mark's mission by giving the majority of their wealth to philanthropy. This act of generosity is known as The Giving Pledge. Paul Allen, Michael Bloomberg, Sara Blakely, and Lyda Hill are a few affluent people associated with The Giving Pledge. Sara Blakely, founder of shapewear brand Spanx, has a mission to help women feel great about themselves. Sara's goal was not to be the youngest self-made woman on Forbes' Billionaire list—which she accomplished—but rather to develop a better undergarment product for women. Mark Zuckerberg and Sara Blakely are truly fulfilled in their professional lives. Regardless of the daily struggles of Facebook or the pressures of running Spanx, both individuals are focusing on their strengths, following their mission, their "North Star."

What is your mission, your North Star? Teaching is very much an emotional profession. Juggling the demands of student achievement, school accountability, safety, community members, financial restraints, and parental expectations requires true dedication. As you rise above these details, be confident in your calling, proud of your arduous efforts, and focus clearly on your North Star.

The Milwaukee Brewers is my favorite baseball team. Each season I attend several games, sometimes cheering them on to victory but too often booing in disgust at their poor play. In any event, regardless of the outcome, watching a baseball game is very enjoyable for me.

While becoming frustrated at the Brewer's performance, I have noticed a significant increase in the way many spectators are violating one of the game's most important unwritten rules. Fans are now constantly moving during innings—regardless of what is happening. The unwritten rule dictates that spectators wait to leave their seats until the end of the inning to prevent obstructing the view of fellow fans. Either this rule is no longer taught or it is just being blatantly ignored.

The same scenario happens at every game I attend. Right as the batter is ready to swing, someone walks in front of me, forcing me to stretch like a warm gummy bear in order to see the pitch. Moments later, as the runner rounds second base and accidently slips, two people step in front of me on their way to the concession stands. This constant movement as the baseball action is taking place is seriously annoying. Why are people standing up in the middle of the action?

I am wondering if these behaviors have started to transfer to other events and activities. Are congregational members standing up to leave in the middle of their pastor's sermon? How much movement is there in a Broadway showing of "Aladdin"? While your niece is blowing out her birthday candles, would you get up and go get a snack?

SUPERHERO EDUCATORS never prevent their students from dreaming big, never put themselves first, never stand between their students and the vision of what their students might become.

Innovative Connections

Most companies exist to make profits. When profits are generated, companies may then explore opportunities to add value to society. This can be accomplished through outright cash donations, merchandise giveaways, or sponsored events. The generosity of the company might then be in turn rewarded through free advertisement, promotions and referrals. Internal leadership of each business decides the amount and frequency of these donations; however, no obligation to be generous exists.

The same spirit applies to a company's ethical behavior. Companies decide upon their values, priorities, and operational practices. Ethical companies do business on the basis of a moral code of conduct, a transparent way of conducting business and implementing corporate social responsibility practices. United Parcel Service (UPS), 3M, MasterCard, Visa, PepsiCo, Intel, Cisco, General Electric, and Microsoft are all widely acknowledged for their ethical behavior. Their ethical reach is seen in their concern for the environment, their commitment to be socially responsible, and efforts to provide corporate transparency. Instituting a code of ethics or a code of conduct ensures that employees are trained in their responsibilities and that their behavior will be positive. Anyone can freely raise integrity concerns through an open reporting process. Annual training on business conduct is a requirement. Ignoring business ethics is as dangerous as leaving profits to chance. Both require planning and proper attention to be sustainable in the 21st century. (Shah, 2017).

For example, the mission statement of UPS includes a commitment to "inspire our people and business partners to do their best, offering opportunities for personal development and success" and to "lead by example as a responsible, caring, and sustainable company making a difference in the communities we serve" ("Mission statement of UPS," 2013). Then again, 3M promises to act "with uncompromising honesty and integrity in everything we do" and to "respect our social and physical environment around the world ("Who we are," 2017). Although a few companies, like Interstate Batteries and Tyson Foods, have clearly faith-based missions, virtually every successful company has a values-based mission statement, but in either case these companies benefit from having a true direction, a North Star. The business is defined as bigger than the profit and losses sheet.

In a similar manner, every school should have a clearly articulated mission statement that allows them to focus on the values that drive their organizations. What is your mission statement as a teacher? Why do you do what you do?

Going to work every day is not simply and solely about a paycheck. Today's employees want more—they want to know they are making a difference in society. GE Healthcare provides an example of this focus on community service. GE Healthcare employs approximately 20,000 workers across the United States. The culture and character of the business encourages employees to give back to their communities. Positive changes in their neighborhoods are seen through GE Healthcare's monetary donations and robust volunteer programs. Reading and mentoring programs, road-side cleaning crews, and marketing experts are a just a few examples of how GE Healthcare is positively influencing its local communities ("GE Recognized as One of the Top 10," 2012).

Once upon a time a man was walking the Italian countryside when he came across twelve resting laborers. Shocked by their sloth, he offered a cash prize to the laziest of them. Upon hearing this, eleven workers jumped up and emphatically made their case. After considering their stories and reasons, he awarded the prize to the twelfth man who hadn't even bothered to get up to plead his case ("Workplace Motivation," 2015). Although humorous, this tale presents a grim view of us as workers. Of course, workers need a fair salary, but I believe they are driven more by the impact of their work than by income. Employees want a voice, opportunities to grow professionally, and the chance to make a difference in our society. Consciously or unconsciously, I believe today's workers are asking themselves, "What is the higher calling that my work allows me to fulfill today?"

Educational Research and Focus

According to the United States Department of Education, there are currently over three million teachers in United States ("Digest of Education Statistics," 2015). Just as every occupation has professionals who excel, countless teachers are demonstrating excellence every day in their classrooms. Unfortunately, too many teachers grudgingly enter their classrooms day in and day out. The teaching profession requires educators who take pride in their work and view their role with great pride.

A key question that is commonly asked as you begin your journey into teaching is, "Why do you want to become a teacher?" Be ready to answer this question. An appropriate response goes beyond, "I love children." The pediatrician, speech pathologist, parent, librarian, and social worker could all say the same thing. Why do you want to enter the profession of *teaching*? Consider your 30-second elevator speech and be prepared to present it. Brian Walter outlined an approach to developing an effective elevator speech he calls, "The WOW, HOW, NOW approach."

1. WOW. Say something intriguing (even puzzling) that will cause the listener to want to learn more. This should be a creative summary of what you do that demands some clarification. Ideally, the prospect's reaction will be to turn his or her head and ask "What does that mean?"
2. HOW. Answer the stated (or unspoken) question and summarize exactly what you do.
3. NOW. Shift into storytelling mode, giving a concrete example from your current professional setting. The key phrase is "Now, for example..." ("Verbal Ping Pong," 2017).

The following is an example of my 30-second elevator speech:

Prospect: So, what do you do?
Me: I train Superheroes.
Prospect: Huh?

Me: I teach people how to become Superhero Educators. Now, for instance, I am working with a school in the city of Milwaukee to train all their teachers to use data more effectively so they can personalize learning and achieve greater student success.

Elevator speeches provide focus and force the author to provide a specific example of what he or she does. Contemplate the impact of your elevator speech. The prospect may be a future parent that wants to volunteer in your classroom, a community member that shares information with the rest of the neighborhood, an administrator looking to brag to the local media, or a funder looking for projects to support. Your elevator speech may influence any number of people.

Notice there is no mention of money or power in an effective elevator speech. **SUPERHERO EDUCATORS** are not driven by money or power but by mission. The importance of the mission overrides any purely selfish motive.

Teachers on a mission make thousands of ethical decisions every day. Consider these two examples.

A school principal distributes his daughter's fundraising forms to all of his faculty and staff during an after-school meeting, bypassing the district's no solicitation policy for fundraising. He jokingly alludes to better faculty and staff evaluations if the fundraising goal is met.

A teacher is planning her daughter's birthday party. She needs to print invitations and mail them to the invited guests. Instead of using the school's paper, ink, and envelopes, she stops at a local office supply store on her way home to print the invitations.

These two educators took two different paths. The difference between the two is their moral compass, their guide for morally appropriate behavior.

SUPERHERO EDUCATORS are equipped with a very clear moral compass. When confronted with making a decision or choosing a direction, the righteous route wins. Educators with this integrity are a wonderful benefit to any school. Schools should do anything they can to retain a teacher with this kind of consistent ethical guide driving clear and ethical decisions.

Working with children and young adults every day places great importance on the value of a moral compass. What keeps your ethics sharp? How are complex decisions analyzed inside of your moral compass? Steven Covey, an expert on leadership and success, examines these important issues ("Moral Compassing," 2009). According to Covey, principles are like a compass. A compass has a true north that is objective and external, that reflects natural laws or principles. Because the compass represents the eternal verities of life, we must develop our value system with deep respect for "true north" principles. Fairness, kindness, dignity, charity, integrity, honesty, quality, service, and patience are some of these inherent principles. Therefore, to maintain our moral sharpness we must constantly put these principles into practice.

For Simon Sinek (2014), integrity means that our words and deeds are consistent with our intentions. A lack of integrity is at best hypocrisy and at worst lying. Integrity is not about being honest when we agree with each other. It is also about being honest when we disagree with each other— or, perhaps even more importantly, when we make mistakes or take missteps. Integrity is particularly important for teachers, since they are usually operating alone on their personal islands, their own separate classrooms.

Teaching can be a very isolating profession. A teacher might arrive at school in the morning and leave at the end of the day without engaging in much adult interaction. A real danger exists when this isolation allows a teacher to relax to the point of unfiltered words and actions—yelling at students, inappropriate language, violence, or even failing to teach because of a recent political election. Ill-considered words and actions can also go so far as to take on a sexual overtone.

Always teach as if someone is videotaping your lessons. Think carefully about what you say and do. Pretend that you and your family will be watching the events of the day unfold on your television that evening. This conscious effort prevents many of the mistakes teachers are vulnerable to because of their isolation in the classroom.

Speaking of being watched, there is actually a good chance that students are recording you. Some students will be using their phone to record your lesson for later review as reliable notes for the upcoming test. Other students will be recording you to see if you make any embarrassing blunders that can be spread around school. Depending on the state you live in, the laws regarding recording people's conversations vary. Knowing the law is not the most relevant part; however, what matters most is your self-control and thoughtful consideration of your words and actions. If what you do would make your mother uncomfortable, it is probably not appropriate in the classroom.

Social media is a remarkable technological innovation. Through social media, people can connect with others around the world. Facebook, Snapchat, Twitter, LinkedIn, Google, YouTube, Pinterest, Instagram, and Tumblr are currently some of the most popular social media sites. Teachers benefit from utilizing social media professionally and personally. However, teachers should carefully consider the boundary between their professional and personal lives. If teachers wish to connect and communicate with students and their families online, they should be careful to keep postings and photos appropriate and professional. Teachers have been fired for posting images in which they are holding alcoholic beverages, using inappropriate language, defaming school personnel, or talking negatively about the students they serve. As absurd as it may seem, a second grade teacher was once fired for sharing on Facebook that he was against dairy farming (Nethers, 2014)—not a wise thing to do in a state like Wisconsin.

As I browse social media and view a variety of teachers' posts, I am astounded at some of the content. Social media posts can be retrieved and reviewed long after you believe they are gone. Based on true examples of teacher posts, educators should avoid:

- Profanity, even if you are frustrated because of commuter traffic or because you were poorly served at one of your favorite restaurants.
- Pictures of you drinking alcohol, even if you want others to know that you are enjoying your night out.

- Complaining about student behavior, even if you are seeking sympathy for your daily struggles.
- Mentioning how sick you are of your co-workers, even if you are.
- Posts that are sexual in nature, even if you think they are funny.

Although your intentions may be innocuous, the results can be damaging. As an example of the lasting negative power of Facebook, remember the case of several students who had their Harvard University acceptance letters revoked because of unacceptable posts to Facebook. Social media posts are not secrets and do not easily go away (Trimble, 2017).

The goal is lofty—to increase student achievement. This means the work is pressing and will involve extra time and energy from every teacher. The idea of service comes to mind as we reflect on how much extra effort teachers are engaged in every day. Providing acts of service to fulfill the mission of your school is necessary—and contagious. Teachers work collaboratively and unselfishly to accomplish the really important tasks.

Teachers are frequently asked to do much more than instruct students—recess and cafeteria duties, after school responsibilities, bus supervision, and professional development workshops. **SUPERHERO EDUCATORS** embrace these roles, willingly going above and beyond, not counting the hours until they can leave the school. "This is not my job" or "I do not get paid for this" are not statements that are heard from **SUPERHERO EDUCATORS**. Embracing the role of a professional educator requires a commitment to be "all in" and present in the moment.

Charlotte Danielson, a leader in teacher evaluation, lists four domains that define effective teaching. An often overlooked element, yet essential to **SUPERHERO EDUCATORS** is the domain titled "Professional Responsibilities" ("The Framework," 2017). Maintaining accurate records, communicating with families, participating in a professional community, growing and developing professionally, and showing professionalism are all part of "Professional Responsibilities." Danielson believes this is one important and accurate measurement of teacher quality. Use this domain as a self-assessment of your commitment to teaching. Analyze your strengths and weaknesses in relationship to "Professional Responsibilities." If you find yourself going above and beyond these responsibilities, you are clearly committed to teaching and the importance of service to your profession. Committing to professional responsibilities definitely makes teaching more than a job.

Knowing you have positively impacted a family or fostered the growth of a student is extremely rewarding. This fulfillment is hard to express in words. It is what keeps teachers recharged and energized to accept new challenges. Awesome teaching transforms lives. In fact, high performing teaching can actually save lives from hopelessness, poverty, and low expectations.

Take pride in the fact that you are a teacher. Not everyone will agree with you or value your teaching vocation, but do not waver. Only you can do what you can do—your impact is truly special. When you begin to doubt the impact of your work, observe other outstanding teachers in action. Study these teachers as they instruct in their classroom and interact with their students. Witnessing great teachers will solidify your work and inspire you to keep going.

Teaching is extremely difficult work but also a tremendous calling. Set a laser focus on your students—they are the reasons you probably went into debt incurring student loans to become a teacher. Your students are worth it! As you focus on students, enjoy teaching. Use humor to engage and motivate students. Reflect on your individual talents and permit your students to see these unique gifts.

One time I developed a series of short skits for an African American Appreciation Night. Included in the skits were numerous jokes that were used to entertain and inform. My students dazzled the crowd as they performed like experienced actors and actresses. Writing the skits, rehearsing the material after school, creating the props, and planning the night were exhausting tasks. This was not in my job description, but it was necessary for student success. Seeing the final performance and the positive reaction of the audience inspired me to take on the same responsibilities for many years to follow.

SUPERHERO EDUCATORS go above and beyond the classroom. They have no choice. It is their calling.

Debriefing Questions

1. What keeps other individuals from signing "The Giving Pledge"?

2. As you go above and beyond in your teaching, how do you balance your home and work life?

3. What are the advantages to businesses for incorporating socially responsible practices?

4. Develop your 30-second elevator speech as a teacher using the HOW, WOW, NOW method.

5. Explain a situation when your moral compass was being tested and you remained steadfast. Conversely, explain a situation when your moral compass was being tested and you wavered in your actions.

6. Evaluate the difficulty of maintaining your moral compass in your current professional setting.

7. Reflect on Chapter 1 Visual: How do you define your calling as an educator?

8. Site an example of a social media post from an educator that you viewed and would consider unacceptable.

9. What is your philosophy for posting to social media? What is acceptable and what is unacceptable?

10. What individual gifts do you possess that led you to your calling?

Notes of Emphasis

CHAPTER 2

Dimension of Drive

Doc McStuffins is a six-year-old doctor with magical tools. She has many toys and stuffed animals that often need her help to feel better. In every case, Doc hangs in there to find a cure. She never lets her friends down and always works hard to fix a problem—she is an unconventional superhero. Doc McStuffins has the desire and the drive to make people feel better. That is what makes her special. **SUPERHERO EDUCATORS** *have a relentless drive to improve instruction for all students.*

Impact Story

ast fall I went to a K&G Fashion Store to pick up a suit coat. I had not purchased a suit coat in several years and wanted something new to wear for the first day of school. I was looking at several different coats, all of which needed to fit my budget. K&G was my store of choice for several reasons. First, the location is close to my house. Second, their prices for suit coats are generally reasonable. Finally, I can get alterations completed on site, which eliminates the need to go to a separate tailor. I try not to enter this store unless I plan on purchasing, since too many times in the past I have been to this store and spent money I did not intend on spending. This store might be my kryptonite.

I am actually not a "suit guy", so I had to figure out why this store brings me back. After reflecting, I am convinced the tenacity of the store clerks ensures customers will have an exciting shopping experience. Their drive for dressing customers is drastically different from any other place I have purchased a suit from in the past. The clerks at K&G check to ensure the suit fits appropriately. That sounds basic, but I have purchased suits from other establishments, and the clerk told me I looked great. I fell for the trap, only to look in the mirror at home and see that my suit really did not fit my frame well.

The clerks at K&G have this magical power. After asking probing questions about suit needs, they come up with at least five choices of suits—with coordinating shirts and ties. Settling on just one option is usually very difficult. I remember one particular instance when I told the clerk I did not really need a shirt and tie to go along with the suit I was buying. The next thing I knew, I had just purchased, you guessed it, a shirt and tie. The clerks do not force customers to buy anything, of course. Their distinctive method appears to be making sure their customers look their best, presenting buyers with a range of stylish options. I am willing to admit, I am hooked. Their drive for customer service has turned me into a loyal customer. I will no longer buy a suit from any other store. Educators, is your drive to teach children so strong that parents will continue to choose your school as option number one?

Innovative Connections

Everything advances over time. As a society, we are always looking for the next big thing. Many people camp out for the latest Samsung phone or the latest Apple iPhone. By 2019, the number of mobile phone users in the world is expected to pass the five billion mark. The mobile phone penetration is forecasted to continue to grow up to 67 percent of the population in the next couple of years ("Number of Mobile Phone Users Worldwide," 2017).

I remember using the rotary phone at my grandparent's house when I was young. Rotary phones required callers to use their finger to spin the dial. Who remembers the phone cord? They were too short, nothing like the freedom of our current cell phones. Calling someone long distance was considered an expensive luxury. Pricey phone bills were the result of reaching out and connecting with your loved ones using long distance calling.

Call waiting soon appeared on the scene. Users now had the ability to click over and say hello to determine which call they wanted to take. Catching a busy signal would no longer be the worst part of the day.

Three-way calling ability arrived shortly after that, and now we could talk to two of our best friends at the same time. All of these luxuries came at a price, and phone bills slowly started to increase.

Back in my day, having a pager meant that you were an official part of the high school power structure. I will never forget the joy I had in attaching my first pager to my belt clip. I cannot thank the genius enough that came up with the idea of having someone text a phone number to my pager.

The next big thing was the cell phone. Do you remember that large device with the delicate antenna? The roaming charge was your worst nightmare. Yikes. Those big batteries were classic—and actually bigger than some cell phones available today.

Who wouldn't want a cell phone that folded and slid smoothly into your pocket? Flip phones provided a certain level of convenience that the first cell phone could not. At the time of this writing, 2017, I still know a few people who own a flip phone. They are resistant to change because of familiarity and view current cell phone features are unnecessary.

After the flip phone came the domination of Apple and Samsung. These are the two current leaders in the cell phone industry. Samsung has a vision for the future entitled "Vision 2020." Samsung Electronics' vision for the new decade is to "Inspire the World, Create the Future." Samsung is committed to developing products and creative solutions "that inspire communities around the world to join our aspiration for creating a better world full of richer digital experiences" (Vision 2020, 2017). When I reflect on this vision, I note how it attempts to make customers feel as if they need the Samsung product to be successful. This is brilliant marketing, and it is easy to interpret how their organization feels about the concept of drive. Samsung wants everyone to experience a better world by using its products.

Apple is the other cell phone giant. According to Roland Alexander, (Alexander, 2017), CEO Tim Cook's mission for Apple includes the following points:

- We believe that we're on the face of the Earth to make great products.
- We believe in the simple, not the complex.

- We participate only in markets where we can make a significant contribution.
- We don't settle for anything less than excellence in every group in the company, and we have the self-honesty to admit when we're wrong and the courage to change.

Reading statements like these, it is hard not to fall in love with Apple. Their drive is to be the best in the world and to convince the general public that they are doing it for us. The people I know who use Apple phones will never use an Android phone. Apple's strategy of brand alliance works.

Educational Research and Focus

The drive of a **SUPERHERO EDUCATOR** is different from the rest of his or her peers. According to Kowal and Brinson (2011), great educators can be created by doing the following:

- Extending teachers' reach beyond traditional classroom boundaries, through redesigns of both organizational structures and job responsibilities that enable great teachers to directly or indirectly reach larger number of students beyond their classroom walls.
- Considering teachers' individual strengths and weaknesses, as well as their overall effectiveness in improving student learning, when conceiving and designing new work roles.
- Designing roles with both students' and teachers' interests in mind, including a clear path between new roles for teachers and the student learning gains they want to achieve.
- Ensuring long-term financial sustainability for what is too often an add-on program by keeping costs in mind from the start.
- Challenging traditional expectations by embarking on a campaign with teachers, administrators, and other stakeholders to clarify the changes to teachers' daily roles and demonstrate the benefits of innovation in this realm for both teachers and students.

The **SUPERHERO EDUCATOR** knows that to be successful in these areas requires drive. In many cases, **SUPERHERO EDUCATORS** assume all teachers have ambition equal to their own and often feel discouraged, frustrated, even crushed when they discover that others in their field do not have the same passion. Although research has identified numerous characteristics of the effective teacher, too often the one characteristic that the research ignores is the individual's drive to be a great educator.

Ms. Oliver is a **SUPERHERO EDUCATOR,** although she would never label herself as such because she is incredibly humble. Ms. Oliver has taught 3rd, 4th, and 5th grade; her current position is school support teacher. She started her educational career as a school secretary. The fact that she made the jump from secretary to school support teacher should tell you all you need to know about her drive.

I have known Ms. Oliver for 15 years and still find it hard to describe her unparalleled drive. It is layered, and we all can learn a great deal from her. She has a passion for ensuring that students of color are provided opportunities to experience success in school. As a student, she suffered in a poor educational environment. Several of her teachers told her she would not be successful. She believed this and developed a negative self-image because of these childhood experiences. Ms. Oliver was driven by those past interactions to be certain she was doing everything in her power to help students feel successful and important. One year, a group of her students joined the flag football team. They were extremely excited to be a part of the extracurricular activity, but that excitement soon turned into disappointment when nobody volunteered to be the head coach.

Ms. Oliver volunteered to coach the team. Flag football is a non-contact sport, but no one gave the message to Ms. Oliver. Her practices were incredibly intense. She ran those practices as hard as Vince Lombardi or Mike Ditka. Ms. Oliver refused to sit back and let the kids suffer because of lack of adult involvement. Outside of being a **SUPERHERO EDUCATOR**, she was also the first female flag football coach in the district.

Ms. Oliver used her military background to establish effective management both on the football field and in her classroom. She understood the connection between an orderly classroom and high student achievement.

Management was the first strength I noticed in Ms. Oliver's classroom. During one of my walk through visits, I heard students verbalizing agreed upon expectations for classroom behavior for the first time in my career. It was awesome and effective. Kafele (2015) suggests that motivating educators to do their best builds a passion for success. When visitors entered Ms. Oliver's classroom, her students could articulate routines and procedures. This was not a dog and pony show. She was teaching her students to become confident leaders.

Transformative leadership is not about wielding authority, rather it is about empowering students to be active participants in a democracy. The classroom becomes a space that embraces critical inquiry, creativity, imagination, and collaboration (Kayler, Demulder, View, & Stribling, 2009). Only a **SUPERHERO EDUCATOR** can accomplish this at a high level. Ms. Oliver utilizes a behavior management strategy often tried but rarely used effectively by others. When she notices a child on the verge of losing his or her temper, she will send that student off with a pass to another classroom to pick up "the purple pen." The pen request will tip off the receiving teacher that the student is in need of walking off energy that was being pent up during the classroom lesson.

I know what you are thinking. You are considering all of the potential problems with this process. First, Ms. Oliver had explicit hallway expectations for her students. With those expectations in place, her students knew how to conduct themselves in the hallway even when she was not present. Second, Ms. Oliver developed teacher relationships with staff that allowed her to enlist destination partners for this project. She knew these selected teachers excelled in building high quality relationships with students. A meta-analysis of the influence of teacher-student relationships on student engagement and achievement indicated that student adjustment was enhanced if the teacher-student relationship was of high quality, especially for at-risk, high-poverty adolescents (Roorda, Koomen, Split, & Oort, 2011).

Third, Ms. Oliver opened up her classroom to students from other classrooms that needed a timeout or to any student that was close to being suspended—one in six African American students have been suspended from school (Losen & Gillespie, 2012). Ms. Oliver knew this data, but she was never comfortable with the message that data sent to all school stakeholders. She would do whatever it took to keep the school suspension rate low.

Many educators celebrate when difficult students are suspended but not Ms. Oliver. She would beg the principal not to suspend her students if they were in trouble. Her goals included implementation of classroom consequences that would be more impactful than out of school suspensions. In the majority of cases, the students feared consequences from her more than the principal. Ms. Oliver had the power.

All of our students will face barriers at one point in time or another. We will also experience barriers as educators. Ms. Oliver expected barriers and accepted those challenges. Good, average and below average teachers often become stuck due to barriers. **SUPERHERO EDUCATORS** like Ms. Oliver refuse to be defined and limited by barriers. When barriers occurred in her classroom, she worked to analyze what caused the barrier. This was significantly different from the actions of her peers who invariably started the blame game once a barrier surfaced. After Ms. Oliver understood the barrier, her next move was to determine what strategy would allow her students to be successful. Ms. Oliver realized that every adjustment to a barrier would not automatically lead to success. If a different strategy was needed, she had no problem regrouping for another attempt to best meet the needs of her students.

There are two jobs I define as the most difficult in a K-12th grade learning environment. Those two jobs are assistant principal and school support teacher. Ms. Oliver was persuaded by her colleagues and school administration to apply for the open school support teacher position. Many candidates applied for the position, but only one person exceeded the hiring criteria. Ms. Oliver's drive and end goal for this position was to secure all the necessary tools for the staff to be successful in the classrooms. According to Gates (2013). The art of teaching is about getting your arms around something as dynamic as a classroom full of young students. They bring a constantly changing set of challenges from their lives at home into the classroom, and teachers are obliged to understand them as individuals, earn their respect, and establish basic discipline—all the while engaging them in academic subject matter. Educators must encourage their students' curiosity for months at a time so that they build a base of knowledge brick by brick, over time.

The greatest challenge for Ms. Oliver would be altering the belief systems of her peer teachers. She worked in the building long enough to know what she would be up against. Her strategy was to win one teacher at a time. Eventually, trust was developed and intentional focus was placed on student achievement.

When you are a **SUPERHERO EDUCATOR**, defying the odds is the norm. The report card ranking for Ms. Oliver's school before she accepted her new role had them ranked at the second lowest academic level. This is a label no educator would want for his or her school. The ranking basically meant that the school as a whole was not meeting expected learning outcomes for students. Ms. Oliver took the challenge as an opportunity to climb the report card ladder. While people around her were pointing fingers at others for the results, or questioning the validity of the results, Ms. Oliver put into place procedures to support teachers and students. One school year later, under the leadership of Ms. Oliver, her school leaped into the second highest category for student achievement—"Exceeds Expectations." This is essentially going from a traditional grade of D to a B. This is practically unheard of on the state report card system. No other school in the district increased as many levels as her school. This was so impressive that the district's central office asked her to share what was done so her efforts could be replicated in other schools.

Some of the teachers would likely be unable to explain how they improved. The positive problem they now faced was figuring out how to maintain those results. Ms. Oliver told me that she felt the pressure. She would like to see the same increases during the next school year. I have confidence, with her drive and determination, her school can show back to back wins. A **SUPERHERO EDUCATOR** would not have it any other way.

As educators we can never forget the power of the influence of our drive. Our influence can only go in three directions: extremely meaningful, forgotten about, or extremely non-effective. Which do you want your legacy to be? How many educators are forgotten or non-effective? When reflecting on the concept of drive, how far away are you from being a **SUPERHERO EDUCATOR?**

Debriefing Questions

1. As an educator, what does *drive* mean to you?

2. How would one of your peers describe your drive to be successful?

3. Briefly describe a person at your school who has **SUPERHERO** drive.

4. Reflect on a teacher who appears to not have a strong drive to be successful. What are two strategies you can suggest to make that person more effective?

5. Reflect on the Chapter 2 Visual: If school educators are driven, how should this affect student learning?

6. Observe five different educators. Record and evaluate how their drives are different from each other.

7. Select three successful businesses. As a teacher, what evidence of drive can you observe and employ from their examples?

8. Reflect on your individual gifts. How can these strengths further your drive as an educator?

9. Compare and contrast. Evaluate a business that you will not patronize because of its lack of drive with one you admire.

10. Do you think drive is taught or is one born with it?

Notes of Emphasis

CHAPTER 3
Infinite Improvement

Superhero Connection

With thousands of high tech gadgets in his body, Inspector Gadget works on continual improvement. He frequently gets caught in peculiar situations. In order to solve problems or offer assistance, Inspector Gadget takes advantage of all the tools he has available. He invariably has in hand the appropriate tool for the dilemma. Tools are at the disposal of all educators to assist in daily situations. Are you utilizing all of your resources and tools as a **SUPERHERO EDUCATOR**?

Impact Story

When I think of continual improvement, I think of my son's soccer journey. I grew up on the big three sports: baseball, basketball, and football. As a new father, I pushed my son into the direction of those big three. He tried baseball, but quickly lost interest. Because of his average size, football was completely out of the question; surprisingly, however, my son actually enjoyed basketball. He played in several leagues and definitely had some talent as a point guard.

Out of the blue in 5th grade, my son decided that he wanted to give soccer a try. I was shocked—after all, this was not one of the big three. Honestly, I tried to talk him out of this new venture. He insisted, so I found a soccer league for him to join. After joining the team, reality hit. Many of the boys on the team had been playing together for several years and had created strong team chemistry. My son wanted to be on the team but lacked the skills to really contribute. As a parent it was difficult to watch his struggle on the field, but my son soon became a true example of continual improvement.

When most kids would have become discouraged or complain about their limited playing time, my son instead worked harder to develop his soccer skills. He practiced his footwork for hours in our backyard and slowly figured out what he could do well. His coaches noticed his extra effort, and my son gradually gained more playing time. With increased time in the game, he started to earn the trust of his teammates. By the time my son was in eighth grade, he had caught up to the skill level of the rest of his peers, which was truly amazing considering his teammates played together since the first grade.

By closing the skills gap with his peers, my son is now a very talented soccer player. He is adept at dribbling the ball through defenders and setting up important assists, often putting his teammates in perfect scoring position. Today, he is one of the leaders on his soccer team. He understands the role of every position on the field. The coach calls my son one of the most coachable athletes on the team. The sport of soccer has helped my son become a valued leader. Those leadership skills will assist him on and off the field. I am not sure where the soccer story will end for my son. The path of continual growth is more fascinating than the wins and losses each week.

Innovative Connections

When I think of continual growth in the business world, I think of the hotel industry. My favorite hotel is the Radisson Blu adjacent to the Mall of America. I admire the style inside of the hotel. It is very modern, and the abstract art is particularly appealing. Most hotel lounge areas are dull, but not here. The lounge is inviting and entices guests into hanging out and talking to strangers.

What I enjoy the most when staying at the Radisson Blu is avoiding the relentless Minnesota winters. Since the hotel is connected to the Mall of America by an indoor walkway, I can bypass going outside on a cold winter day. My many pleasant experiences at the Radisson Blu motivated me to dig a little deeper into the desired hotel experience and how the hotel industry is always evolving. The first common theme I noticed when researching the hotel industry was how continual improvement is needed to stay competitive.

Any organization that is serious about continual improvement will focus on feedback from its customers. Like Radisson, Marriott has achieved success due to a strategic management commitment to employee empowerment to enhance customer service and drive revenue. Through development programs and employee enrichment, Marriott's management recognizes that its most important resource, its employees, is the key to success in the service-driven lodging industry (Ahmad, Walter, & Sherman, 2016).

Hotel staff routinely ask questions to ensure the customer is satisfied. How was your stay? How can I help you? Do you want your bed sheets changed? Once I had a complaint about the cleanliness of a room in which I stayed in Tennessee. I was too upset to talk to the manager. Instead, when I made it home, I gave the general manager a call. After I explained the situation, she told me the hotel would refund all of my expenses. She also offered me a discount on my next stay. She concluded by indicating she would visit the hotel herself and have a conversation with the manager concerning the matter. I was thankful and honestly felt convinced that she was interested in exceeding my expectations, but, perhaps even more importantly, she was determined to develop continual improvement for that particular hotel.

The hotel industry also responds quickly to written feedback. "By responding to negative reviews, a firm signals that it cares about its customers and will continue to do so in the future, thus enhancing perceptions of its character. By demonstrating both capability and good character, a firm can enhance its reputation" (Rose & Blodgett, 2016). Hotel guests always have an opportunity to provide feedback to management. On one occasion, I provided written feedback to housekeeping, which immediately made changes based on my feedback. The housekeeper even left her name and expressed her appreciation for the feedback. I felt like a personal connection was established, and I am convinced my hotel experience improved each day. Hotels are always seeking to improve themselves.

As an example of continuous improvement, major hotel chains such as Hilton and Marriott are now allowing guests to use their smartphones to access hotel rooms and hotel services. At these specific chains, guests can use their smartphones as room keys, unlocking room doors and guest-only areas such as fitness rooms and pools (Mandelbaum, 2015).

The hotel where I stayed during the time I wrote this chapter had signs located throughout the building highlighting areas that were under construction, informing the guests that they were working hard to improve the overall hotel experience for the benefit of their clientele. The culminating effect of these continual improvements efforts establishes brand loyalty. When earning customer loyalty, there are no second chances. Never assume a customer will cut you slack because you've got a long history together. To earn loyalty, you must constantly prove to the customer that the relationship is crucial (James, 2013).

This is loyalty in a manner that establishes deep connections to the traveler. I know many people, including my wife, that insist on staying at a certain hotel chain regardless of the city they are visiting. Once loyalty is established and a particular hotel exceeds her expectations, she will book that hotel repeatedly. Once brand allegiance has been created, customers will stay exclusively with that brand.

Educational Research and Focus

Educators frequently seek out the help of external experts and consultants who can provide professional development, offer stimulating new ideas, and even offer extensive plans for change to an entire school community. Professional development is absolutely essential for continual improvement. School stakeholders argue passionately over whose opinion or which strategy is most appropriate for advancing their school's mission. Strategizing the utilization of data from assessments is one way to generate infinite improvement.

One of the many assessments used in districts around the country is the Measures of Academic Progress (MAP). Students take the MAP assessments three times per school year—in the fall, winter, and spring. Student scores fall into three categories: red, which means standards are not met, yellow, which indicates needed growth, and green, which is the desired goal. This process also provides a color ranking for individual classrooms, grade levels, and the entire school.

Bush K-8th School was located in the heart of Milwaukee. Based on their MAP scores, they had an overall yellow ranking. Interestingly enough, however, the school's 1st-5th grades were averaging green in math and reading, while the next three grades were averaging red on those same measures. After reviewing this information, questions began to surface from administration. Is the data skewed because of behavior, attendance, or lack of student's prior knowledge? Are the teachers teaching more effectively in the 1st-5th grades? Do the middle school teachers truly understand the content they are teaching? Do the students take the MAP assessments seriously? Do the middle school teachers teach with rigor? Do the middle school teachers lack effort? Do the parents understand the importance of the MAP assessments? Was the problem the fault of the principal for not holding teachers accountable?

After extensive discussion, the district administrators determined that the cause of the low scores was the lack of holding the middle school teachers accountable, the lack of middle school teachers understanding the content they teach, and the middle school teachers not following the prescribed pacing guide. The school principal, however, felt the problem had to do more with the entire school community not taking the MAP assessments seriously.

Under the Every Students Succeed Act, schools have an expectation of accountability and action to influence positive change. Consequently, in collaboration with the middle school's teaching staff—which to her surprise she found both enthusiastic and committed—the principal developed an action plan that included a number of specific steps.

First, the staff agreed to develop several different types of incentives based on MAP assessment results, including a prize for the classroom that made the highest gains in math and small incentives for individual students that showed the highest percentage gains in reading. Those efforts were aimed at encouraging students to take the assessments seriously rather than randomly guessing answers to the questions. The hope was that if students took the test with more focus, their scores would increase.

Second, everyone agreed that each middle school teacher would implement additional, purposeful intervention sessions for reading and math. Although the school did follow the Response to Intervention guidelines, implementation was superficial. In reading, the teachers committed to additional sessions with students who were on the verge of being proficient, while in math, they focused on those students who struggled the most with MAP assessments.

Third, the staff concurred that the MAP assessments needed to be positively promoted. Middle school learners are motivated to read by their perceptions and value of the content they are reading (Pitcher et al., 2007). Public address announcements were made well in advance of the assessments. To make sure parents were aware of upcoming MAP assessments, school officials sent messages through an auto dialer.

Fourth, the school scheduled middle school students last on the assessment schedule, which allowed maximum academic instruction time.

Fifth, the decision was made to have a respected, no nonsense teacher administer the assessment in two classrooms that tended to have behavior problems rather than have their homeroom teachers conduct the tests. As Ma and Crocker (2007) have shown, schools with better classroom behaviors have higher student achievement rates compared to schools with challenging behavior concerns. The principal hoped that this would provide a better testing environment for students and present the students with the best chance of success.

Sixth, the principal visited each class before the students took the MAP assessments to share expectations and set targeted aims. This kind of goal setting established specific criteria for behavior targeted for change and the time frame allotted for meeting those criteria (Miltenberger, 2008). The principal wanted each student to claim success in advance and to let students know that she supported their efforts, something that had not been adequately communicated in the past.

Lastly, the principal personally met with every 6th-8th grade student to discuss the importance of the MAP assessment, to review each student's previous scores and to set goals for the upcoming assessment. She called this her "Middle School Motivation Tour." This increased the willingness of the students to do their best—a key component for them to do well in school—and brought their behavior more in line with that of successful students. Those who focus, do not waste time in class, are engaged in the lesson, and love to learn are typically more successful (Palmer, 2007).

As a result of these interventions, each grade level saw increased scores on the MAP, particularly in the middle school grade levels, the primary target of the interventions. From an unacceptable red rating on the previous testing cycle, the middle school average was now a high yellow. As a consequence of this improvement, the entire school missed moving out of yellow by a mere 1%. Although the principal was disappointed to have narrowly missed the ultimate goal of the green rating, the results were nevertheless a real victory for the school, giving teacher morale a needed boost and providing a great springboard for the upcoming school year.

SUPERHERO EDUCATORS never stop improving. They may pause, realign, and evaluate, but they never stop moving forward. Phil Knight (Knight, 2016) discusses this idea as he built NIKE into a billion dollar business. And to those who urge entrepreneurs to never give up? Don't ever stop.

Hats off to the staff at the Bush K-8th School for strapping on their **SUPERHERO EDUCATORS'** capes and doing what it takes to meet the needs of students through their efforts to continually improve.

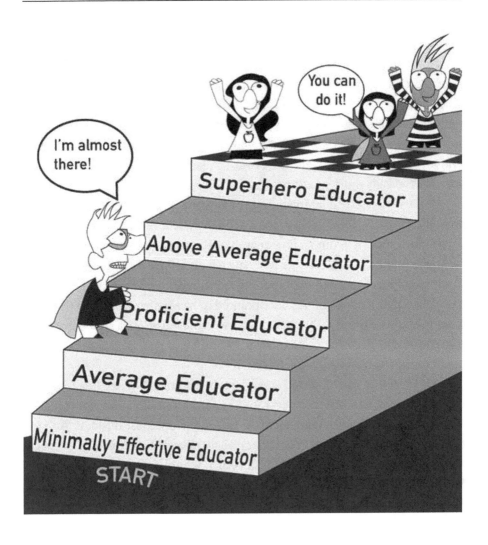

Debriefing Questions

1. Can you engage in continual improvement without increasing test scores? Explain.

2. Too much emphasis is made on improving test scores. Agree or Disagree. Defend your answer.

3. What do you think is the best way to motivate students for their continual improvement?

4. How can teachers review their teaching practices to determine if they are improving?

5. Should a teacher need to be reminded to focus on continual improvement? Explain.

6. How would one of your peers describe your drive for continual improvement?

7. Reflect on the Chapter 3 Visual: Briefly describe a person on your staff that has made continual improvements. How did he or she do it?

8. Briefly describe a person on your staff that has not made continual improvements. What are they doing wrong?

9. Observe five different educators. Compare and contrast their responses to the following question: What have you done in the last month to improve as an educator?

10. List three businesses that embody continual improvement.

Notes of Emphasis

CHAPTER 4

Robust Risk-Taking

Superhero Connection

As a founding member of the Justice League of America, Aquaman rules the waters. Aquaman is king of Atlantis, communicating with fish by telepathic means and controlling their actions. Living in and out of the water, Aquaman must decide when to invest his energies and powers. Taking calculated risks is a true strength of Aquaman. How can you take professional risks to further your goals?

Impact Story

Adidas once dominated the athletic shoe and clothing manufacturing industry. Seeing Jesse Owens in a pair of Adidas shoes sprinting to the finish line in the 1936 Olympics caused fans around the world to yearn for their own pair. Flashing Adidas shoes meant you were serious about your body and your sport.

Then along comes Phil Knight. Phil loved running and teamed up with a university track coach to develop a premier running shoe, which led to the formation of the company NIKE. What gave Phil the courage to take on Adidas and commit to a tremendous risk by starting a company based on a running shoe? Remember, the year was 1964 and few people equated running with recreation and enjoyment. Outside of track and field enthusiasts, running shoes were not a priority for most people. Surely, there was little thought that 30 billion dollars of yearly revenue could possibly be obtained from a risky business venture based on athletic footwear and sports apparel.

As teachers, we need to take professional risks. We need to be bold. At some point in your education or career, you may have been asked, "Who was your favorite teacher? Why?" These questions usually result in responses that resonate with unrelenting love and very high standards of excellence.

"I hated math, but because of Ms. Taylor I soared in accounting."

"No one disrespects Mr. Redding because they want to hear his engaging stories and applications to real life."

"Mrs. Ricardo gets to know us personally, which makes me want to try harder in class."

"I tried hard because I did not want to disappoint Mr. Jefferson."

Favorite teachers lovingly often go out on a limb to stretch their students, leading them to find success in critical thinking and problem solving. Developmentally, the experiences that can be the most potent are the ones that stretch or challenge people. Comfort is the enemy of growth and continued effectiveness. Challenging experiences create disequilibrium, causing people to question the adequacy of their skills and approaches. Creative problem solving always involves risk but great educators know it is necessary when there is a discrepancy between what exists and the desired situation and often involves finding a solution that is either unknown or not commonly used (Drapeau, 2014).

Innovative Connections

Autonomous driving is a great example of professional risk-taking. Reading a newspaper or eating your breakfast on the morning commute as your car drives itself seems like a giant leap of faith. Cars that drive themselves are being mastered at places like Google, Tesla, Ford, and MIT. The benefits of energy savings, reduction of accidents, and faster commute times will make this risk worthwhile. Although the invention of autonomous cars will likely have a negative impact on certain jobs, opportunities will also abound. Since drivers will no longer be exclusively focused on driving, various enhancements like food service and video might be possible. Will a workstation inside a vehicle be developed to replace the traditional office? (Hyatt, 2017). Ford Motor Company, which was founded over a hundred years ago, is risking millions of dollars in developing autonomous driving technology—a demonstration of the company's staying power.

Risk taking offers personal and professional benefits, but leaders must do their research to fully grasp the realities of all possible outcomes. JetStream Federal Credit Union CEO, Jeanne Kucey, knows the importance of fully understanding the consequences of risk-taking. "While I'm definitely a risk taker, at the same time, I do my homework and understand the importance of implementation and follow through. You can't just throw out a bunch of ideas without seeing the whole process of a project and what the end should be or look like" (Zeilinger, 2013).

SUPERHERO EDUCATORS know they must take professional risks to achieve great results. They also realize that before they attempt to confront daunting challenges, they must study and analyze all potential outcomes. Collaboration and networking are crucial as risk-taking becomes part of the educator's routine.

Educational Research and Focus

Going out on the proverbial limb and taking a chance is always a gamble. You will run the risk of loss. Educational risks mean pushing back against the status quo, attempting a new approach, or finding an innovative solution for the success of all students. Taking a risk is not a one-time event but rather a mindset that teachers continue to refine as they make learning relevant. An educational risk can be unpleasant, even scary, but try to maximize success by taking a calculated approach. The focus is always on the students and the mission of the school. The quickest way to jeopardize the risk is to lose focus.

SUPERHERO EDUCATORS are experts in classroom management. Properly managing a large group of unique individuals requires tremendous energy and thought. You need to successfully manage the complexity of a classroom environment and ensure students achieve at their highest possible academic levels. But taking professional risks in your classroom is imperative. The arrangement of your classroom is an easy starting point. Develop an intentional flow in your classroom with the desks, resources, and materials organized to maximize learning.

When I was a student, straight rows of desks were the norm. The teacher's desk stood upfront and every student faced the same direction. As I started teaching, I quickly realized I did not care for desks placed in rows at all. My goal was to get from one student's desk to another's quickly and easily to work with them individually. With the desks in traditional rows, I was routinely bumping into students and their chairs and discovered that it simply took too long to navigate my classroom the way I desired. The only way I could avoid those pitfalls was to address each student by talking across the room, over their heads, like the teachers that plant themselves at the front of the class. I found this a barrier to forming and fostering those important personal relationships.

Purchasing tables and chairs for the classroom seemed like a risky but ideal solution. This provided superb flexibility with grouping and also granted me the ability to cluster my students. A few skeptical colleagues questioned how I would be able to control students if they were sitting in groups. My response was and is always, "I am going to teach my students, not control them."

Many people will not move forward or take action because of fear. The fear of the slippery slope is real. Apprehensive teachers will resist giving up rows because students might talk louder, may not pay attention in class, might copy off of their neighbor's paper, or fail to remain focused on the teacher. But you are the teacher, you control the environment!

This slippery slope argument is also used when discussing student group work. Handing out worksheets and compelling students to complete them independently is fine in small increments. Making this your lesson plan for the day is unacceptable. In the 21st century, we know that students must be able to collaborate and participate in group learning. The demands of their future employment require this preparation. Practicing and implementing group work during the day aptly prepares our students. The risk factor here, of course, will be students who try to cheat, consume time with talking, and allow another student to do all of the work. However, these obstacles are not so overwhelming that they should prevent you from implementing group work in your classroom. With consistency of expectations, these issues will be kept to a minimum.

Educators model this type of learning for their students as well. Teaching is no longer a task that we undertake independently. Instead, we are members of a professional learning community, working collaboratively with our grade-level teams, content departments, or whatever configuration our schools embrace (Hall & Simeral, 2015). Take the risk and allow your students the same benefits of collaboration that you enjoy with your peers.

Imagine a first grade teacher walking down a school hallway. He spots several eighth graders lingering by their lockers and overhears them discussing inappropriate behaviors. The risk-adverse teacher will rationalize: "That is not my group of students; therefore, I am not going to get involved." But the teacher who is able and willing to take a professional risk demands that this behavior be addressed immediately. It is an act of love. When you really love others, you want what is best for them and desire that they are successful. You must address this behavior in the hallway because you truly care for all students, and the behavior of these particular students involves actions that are inconsistent with your school's mission.

SUPERHERO EDUCATORS are content experts. Although it is not possible to know everything, as a lifelong learner you embrace knowledge and are in constant pursuit of it. As you master your content, go ahead and take a risk with your teaching methods. If you feel lecture is the best way to deliver the specific content, try mixing in some group work and feedback questions. Use technologies like PowerPoint and the Internet. Include personal stories and applications. Remember, teaching is not about your comfort level, about mindlessly copying worksheets to distribute. The goal of your teaching is to reach all students, show progress, and achieve positive results.

At one school, I witnessed a classroom where the teacher was supposed to be teaching math and science, but the classroom was void of science equipment. After I addressed several questions, the teacher confessed that she did not like science. This discomfort led her to only teach science when it could be integrated into her math lessons. This fails to meet the students' needs and shortchanges the value of science. Rollins (2017) agrees that learners tend to achieve more and remember concepts better when they can engage in hands-on, collaborative learning. Creating more active learners is not about teachers doing less but rather asking their students to do more. Instructional teaching plans should be thoughtful and personalized, serving as essential guides. Student-centered instruction is not less organized but more deliberate in action. Instruction that is not thorough in preparation and lacks organization can actually reduce student achievement.

The ideal school partnership with a parent and a teacher is one of mutual respect and admiration. Parents are the primary educators of their children—teachers assist in the process. For a variety of reasons, the partnership between parents and teachers sometimes breaks down. **Superhero Educators** understand that there is nothing wrong with going out on a limb and asking parents for insights into their child. "Alex becomes distracted very easily when we are in our group discussions for science. Do you notice this type of distracted behavior at home? If so, what are some strategies you utilize to help?" Asking for guidance shows that you respect the role of parents in their child's learning.

Developing this kind of a relationship with parents is a professional risk because you are opening up to parents and revealing that you do not know everything. This approach is more desirable than acting like you know what is best for every child and leaving the impression that parents are making your job difficult.

Seeking parental feedback involves personal and professional risk but consider the positive benefits. Clark Howard is a popular consumer advocate regularly appearing on national radio and television. His mission is to help people "save more, spend less, and avoid rip-offs". One segment of his show is called "Clark Stinks." During this portion of the show, Clark reads messages posted by listeners who think he missed the mark or was just plain wrong on a topic. Clark addresses these on the air by responding to their concerns. Taking this risk only makes Clark's show better and his future responses more accurate by holding himself accountable.

This approach to feedback can be accomplished with parents as well. Ask parents where you are missing the mark or what could be improved. Feedback can be generated through a survey. The results can remain private but nonetheless offer valuable data. This does not mean that you need to change something every time a parent complains, but it does show you are listening. The solicited feedback may strengthen your teaching philosophy. For example, a parent may complain that there is too much homework for her daughter because her involvement in club volleyball limits her time. In this situation you may check your school's homework policies and review the research, examine your current policy and nevertheless come to the conclusion that your policy is right on target. Receiving parent feedback forces you as a professional to fine tune your work and articulate specific reasons for your approach to teaching.

On the other hand, if a parent shares a wonderful story about how his son has advanced a reading level because of your "NBA Challenge Project," you will naturally want to continue the project, even though it involves countless hours of work. Requesting parent feedback is scary because we all desire positive approval from others—but go ahead and take the risk! Trust that parents will appreciate the openness. You may even begin eliminating blind spots you were not aware of previously as an educator.

The same can be said for student feedback. Let students evaluate you as a teacher. Did alarm bells just go off in your head? Several worries probably came to mind immediately. "What if students say I am a terrible teacher?" "Do students really know what is in their best interests?" "Don't all students like the easy teachers, the teachers with little expectations?" In spite of these natural questions, do not minimize the power of student insight. Being together for over seven hours a day five days a week, students will quickly understand your personality—the good and the bad. As with parental feedback, you still hold the power in the classroom. You are simply going to analyze student reflections to assist in your professional growth.

Think of the money and resources that are spent today on collecting feedback. Restaurants routinely offer free food or drinks for completed surveys. Retailers enter the consumer in a drawing for prizes if they provide solicited comments. The importance of this feedback is definitely not lost on these companies. You, likewise, have a captive audience to present you with real time assessments. Take the professional risk and find ways to attain honest parent and student feedback.

Technology is a terrific teaching tool. Today, the majority of teachers are efficiently using an electronic grade book, taking attendance online, and uploading information to their school website. When I started teaching over twenty years ago, I had to write out by hand many of my worksheets and assignments. Look how far we have come! I remember being able to refer students to only one picture of the Egyptian pyramids—the one in the textbook. These days, a student can view thousands of pictures of the pyramids, read current research, and even talk directly to an expert on pyramids halfway around the world through video conferencing. The power of technology to influence our classrooms is absolutely astounding.

In spite of the obvious power of technology, many teachers strongly resist integrating technology into their classrooms. Some teachers feel that students spend too much time in front of computer screens anyway. Some assume that if students are turned loose on the Internet, they will just look at inappropriate sites and pictures. Some teachers, fearful that students know more about high tech gadgets than they do, feel uncomfortable utilizing technology.

SUPERHERO EDUCATORS take professional risks! Embracing technology and trying new tools that benefit students involves the teacher who is willing to try something new. We are preparing students for jobs that do not yet exist. The skills of collaboration, creativity, problem solving, critical thinking, and persistence are altogether essential and can be significantly enhanced by the appropriate use of technology.

The art of teaching is indisputably complex. Your role as a teacher is to show progress and growth with all students. The variations in student motivation, interests, talents, and backgrounds are immense. Some children are lucky enough to walk through the school doors having been exposed to frequent and meaningful conversations with adults, educational enrichments and camps, maybe even the rich experiences of travel. Others appear in our classrooms with limited vocabulary, a background of severe poverty, or poor behavioral choices. The ultimate goal is to challenge *all* children, to achieve growth in *all* students. The risk educators need to take is never giving up on any student. Take that professional risk and expect each and every student to succeed. Remember, you are a **SUPERHERO EDUCATOR.**

The summer of my fourth year of teaching, I was handed a file on every student that was entering my classroom in the fall. The children's previous teacher thought he was doing me a favor by providing these summaries. Quickly and politely, however, I declined the information, explaining that each student had an entire summer to mature and should start fresh in the fall with their new teacher. I refused to be influenced by someone else's biased thoughts and opinions of the past. I wanted to greet every student with strong expectations and love. Fight for all students and advocate for those students when no one else will stand up for them. Again, teaching is truly complex, but that is why you are needed so much. If teaching meant working with only exceptionally smart students and involved parents, **SUPERHERO EDUCATORS** would not be needed to save the day. But you *are* needed. You are needed to achieve success with all students.

One final risk that I strongly encourage you to engage is pursuing additional funding opportunities for your school. You are likely to find that your community supports local schools and wants to assist when possible. Ask local businesses for donations and products to further your classroom goals. For example, suppose you are creating a play based on your English instruction. This is a great opportunity to ask around for assistance. Go to a local coffee shop and request a donation of drinks to welcome parents to the show. Visit your local restaurants and ask for appetizers or desserts for the play's reception. Grocery stores or fast food restaurants may provide paper products. A larger company may donate money for props and costumes.

Asking for donations and funding is a professional risk. It is difficult to ask people for money and goods. You might be told to just go away, but the payoff is worth the risk. With additional funds, you will be able to expand and increase learning inside and outside of the classroom. Use your imagination and regard your community as proud supporters of your work. In return you can proudly promote these companies and businesses as partners in student achievement.

Taking professional risks will certainly benefit your students. Whether you are seeking feedback, implementing new technology, or seeking out of the box partnerships, your risk-taking efforts make you a **SUPERHERO EDUCATOR**.

Debriefing Questions

1. Define the idea of educational risk.

2. Are taking educational risks necessary? Explain.

3. From your experiences as a student, how did your teachers take professional risks with classroom management?

4. Give an example of the slippery slope argument.

5. Describe how you build parental support as a high-performing teacher.

6. Being open to feedback from students, teachers, and community members is important. What fear do you have about receiving this feedback?

7. List examples of technology that can be integrated into your classroom.

8. Explain what you do when students do not follow your classroom rules or struggle with motivation to learn.

9. What ideas do you have to secure additional funding for your classroom?

10. Reflect on the Chapter 4 Visual: What causes teachers to avoid educational risks?

Notes of Emphasis

CHAPTER 5
Power Planning

Superhero Connection

Captain America has become one of the most popular superheroes. Captain America is very strategic when using his indestructible shield. At times Captain America throws his shield to thwart the bad guys. At other times, the shield is used for his own protection. Interestingly, the shield is always in position, ready to be used. Can you imagine what would have happened to Captain America if he was disorganized and misplaced this necessity?

Impact Story

Most educators look forward to the end of the school year. Many educators dream about sleeping in on a sunny summer morning. Some have part time jobs, while others have exciting vacation plans. I look forward to summer break because it allows me to spend quality time with my own kids and my lovely wife.

After one particularly stressful school year, vacation time was genuinely needed. My wife and I decided to get away for a few days in July, but we were unsure of where we should go. We narrowed the list to three finalists: Las Vegas, Minneapolis, and New York City (NYC). Each destination had the right ingredients for a perfect vacation. After much deliberation, the executive decision was made to take a bite out of the Big Apple.

New York is absolutely my favorite place in the world. I love the fast pace, the culture, the stores, and the food in New York City. My wife loves sightseeing and shopping. On our first day in NYC we checked off one of the top items on our list by adventuring into the Macy's Department Store in Herald Square. We woke up bright and early that morning, ate a quick breakfast, then caught a cab and headed to Macy's.

We spent a great deal of time looking at purses and perfumes, which made up all of the first floor. We hopped on an escalator in search of the floor that housed the women's shoes. Thankfully, we needed to go up only one flight. I could see the sparkle in my wife's eyes, like a kid in a candy shop, as we arrived to what we anticipated would be the promised land of footwear. I am sure my wife had a magic number in her mind of how many pairs she hoped to purchase.

Something really strange happened, however, as we stepped off the escalator. The sheer disarray and disorganization of the shoe department made my wife's emotions plummet from utter excitement to downright disgust. Shoes were strewn literally everywhere. Macy's shoe department looked like a scene from a war movie. Most of the shoes were not displayed nicely in racks, as one would expect. We had to climb over mountains of shoes just to walk down the aisles. I had never seen anything like this before. To my surprise, numerous customers were indifferently digging through all the piles, hoping to find that special pair. No workers were in sight to organize the mess.

We did enjoy the rest of our week in New York City, although the Macy's shoe department was a memorable disappointment with its lack of orderliness and structure.

Innovative Connections

Black Friday shopping is something I simply refuse to do. In 2015, more than 154 million consumers shopped in stores and online that day (Disis, 2016). Although I would have liked to have taken advantage of some of the sales, the hassle and disorder was not worth the effort. Although buying a promoted item might have resulted in a non-monetary gain—the feeling of getting a bargain—such a purchase might also result in a non-monetary loss—having to shop at an inconvenient time. Such "double-edged" aspects of promotions are evident on Black Friday. Especially frustrating would be making the effort to shop at an inconvenient time and still be unable to purchase the promoted items due to stock outs (Lennon, Johnson, & Lee, 2011).

The last time I dared shop on Black Friday was at Toys-R-Us. A gazillion shoppers squeezed into the store, almost certainly well beyond the building's legal occupancy. Frantic sale hunters were stuck in the aisles, unable to reach that last must-have electronic item. Too many people meant roadblocks everywhere. The checkout lines were impossibly long. People were bumping each other with shopping carts. I later saw on the news several fights actually erupted. Never again!

The previous year we went to Kohl's Department Store on Black Friday, which provided a totally different shopping experience. The store was obviously prepared and properly staffed. Cart traffic followed an obvious plan, allowing shoppers to move freely throughout the store. The checkout procedure had been streamlined, and customers did not have to wait in an excruciatingly long line to pay for their deals. By being organized, Kohl's offered a surprisingly pleasant Black Friday shopping experience. Even after the mad rush of penny pinchers, the store was still clean, and merchandise was not tossed all over the place.

In spite of the madness inherent in Black Friday shopping, effective organization can bring order to even the most potentially chaotic situations.

Educational Research and Focus

All **SUPERHERO EDUCATORS** are organized. Some seem to have been born with a natural gift for organization, while others must make real effort to achieve excellence this category. However organization is accomplished, classroom veterans agree that a primary-grade classroom that lacks good organization is flirting with chaos and organizing a classroom must begin long before the first day of school (Avitabile, 2007). Being organized might just be the one variable that could make or break your career. The objective in what follows is to guide you in this quest to become purposefully planned and organized.

First of all, keep your desk neat. To a student, parent, visitor or colleague, this could be the first impression of you as an educator. We know that first impressions can be unfair, but let's be honest. The very first thing I look at is the teacher's desk. Fair or unfair, I will make some basic assumptions about the organization of a teacher by the appearance of his or her desk. More often than not, my first impression turns out to be correct.

If you wonder why this is so important, the answer is very simple. Organization is an indicator of a teacher's future success or failure. Students learn from your every move. They need a positive model of organization, which should start with the teacher. When students are in a classroom with an educator who is organized, just being in the room exposes them to a blueprint of how they too can be organized. Efficiency is golden for an educator but nearly impossible to achieve without organization.

Nothing is worse than losing a student's work because you cannot locate it in the piles of junk on your desk. Students recognize disorganization and will definitely play the game of blaming you for losing their work, happily adding you to "the dog ate my homework" list of excuses. Perhaps even worse is misplacing that document that needs to be turned in to the principal that afternoon—an embarrassing and completely avoidable experience.

If organizing your desk is a struggle for you, get help. Talk to teachers who are known for their organization. Go on Amazon and search for books on organization. With effort and commitment, your colleagues—and, more importantly, your students—will soon marvel at how efficiently you stay on top of everything.

After organizing your desk, get your classroom in order. As an educator, you will be judged on the organization of your classroom. Have you ever walked into a classroom that was in complete disarray? Did you notice the disorganized piles of papers, the scattered library books, the random art supplies, the dirty pencil shavings ground into a stained rug? How did you feel? Were you stressed? Anxious? Did you want to get out of there as fast as humanly possible? Would you want your kids to be educated in that classroom?

I have discussed how children need a model for organization. This goes far beyond the teacher's desk. I am a firm believer that classrooms without methodical organization lead to lower student achievement and increased behavior problems. If there is trash on the floor, pick it up. Your school's custodial staff should not be the first line of defense against messes.

You have basically two options to set the tone of your classroom and maintain order. Either clean up after your students or teach your students to clean up after themselves. Which makes more sense to you? I suggest that you have students take an active role in keeping your classroom orderly. Cox (2016) discusses how to involve students in the process of doing that:

1. Assign one student in a row or in a group of desks the job of pre-monitor. His or her job is to check the desks in the section before class even starts. If your pre-monitor finds anything, he or she reports it to the monitor.

2. Assign another student the job of monitor. His or her job is to check the desks and the surrounding area after each lesson or activity. If the monitor finds anything amiss, he or she must politely ask the student to set things right. If the student doesn't listen, the monitor then reports to the teacher for further instructions.

3. Assign a third student the job of checker. His or her job is to check anything that the pre-monitor or monitor missed throughout the day.

Such a system should make the learning environment more functional for both the teacher and the students. A student-friendly process such as this also helps to build student accountability for cleanliness.

Every school seems to have one teacher that stuffs miscellaneous clutter all over the classroom, arguing that he or she knows where everything is. If you ever hear this kind of statement, politely challenge this because it is almost certainly not true.

Once you have purposefully cleaned up the clutter and reorganized your classroom and its contents, it is time to design substitute teacher plans. One way to respect the field of education is to be ready with plans for your possible absence. It is your professional responsibility to plan in advance to ensure your class runs as smoothly as possible when you are not there. Both new and even veteran teachers sometimes struggle with knowing how to prepare for a substitute teacher. The key is to create a substitute binder that includes everything a substitute teacher would need to know to effectively run the classroom in your absence. Your binder should of course present the information in a way that makes it easy to find specific details as needed (Durgin, 2016).

I can hear some of you thinking, "I will never be absent!" or "I never get sick." You may not plan on being absent, but emergencies do happen. Providing lesson plans and such necessary information as class lists, procedures, and schedules is imperative. As a former school principal, nothing made me more upset than receiving a call from a substitute informing me that the classroom teacher did not leave behind any plans. The most common response I heard from the teacher the next day was, of course, that he or she had not expected to be absent.

Do the right thing and plan in advance. Most classrooms do not function well when the usual teacher is not there. Help your students and the substitute teacher by being exceptionally prepared. Regardless of your thoughts about substitute teachers and their abilities to teach a lesson, you must leave organized plans for them to follow.

Now that the substitute folder rests on your neatly organized desk, you are ready to begin the process of creating your lessons. Regard your lesson plan book as your bible, your guidebook, and your roadmap all rolled into one. Lesson planning allows you to develop, with purpose, the content to be covered daily. On the flip side, it outlines your reflections at the end of each school day to determine whether or not learning goals, intentions, and criteria were met. A lesson plan maps the course of instruction for one or more classes. It is the recipe for the day's exciting learning (Dabbs, 2012).

I personally loved lesson planning and aimed to consistently have plans ready one month in advance. Obtaining all the appropriate resources for challenging concepts or interesting activities often needed this extra time. This would be impossible to accomplish without effective lesson planning. New teachers should not fall for the rationalization of their more experienced counterparts who claim they do not need lesson plans. This is simply not true. **SUPERHERO EDUCATORS** do not accept that type of thinking.

I would not want to work with any educator that concludes that he or she is above planning. That person is disrespecting our profession, but more importantly, they are disrespecting the students. Although the veteran teacher may have notable experience in a certain subject area, each year there are new students with unique needs. Content, available resources, and expectations change over time.

SUPERHERO EDUCATORS like to challenge themselves. Repeating the same lesson over and over, year after year, is not a challenge and will not inspire greatness. Who wants to be an average educator?

After you have become comfortable with your lesson plan book and are getting ahead of the game by being intentional in your planning process, it is wise to establish a predetermined, clearly communicated plan for homework assignments. Teacher expectations can differ from parent expectations, which can also differ from district expectations. I have worked in districts where homework was part of the student's academic grade and districts that did not allow this practice. Please be mindful of the homework policy of your district.

If your district policy allows homework to be factored into the grade, your first decision will be to figure out how much of a percentage homework will account for in the final grade. Your second decision should be how much homework will be assigned and how it will be graded. Finally, you must consider what happens when a student has mastered the concept that will be practiced in the homework but does not actually complete the assignments.

If your district does not allow homework to be factored into a grade, you must determine how you will manage the homework expectations. When some children are aware that homework is not a component of their grade, a strong probability exists that these students will stop completing their homework. Consider the value of the homework you give and make sure that your intentions go beyond simply wanting them to practice or be prepared for the next lesson. Keep in mind the importance of engaging (and maintaining) a love of learning and a curiosity about life and the world beyond the subject itself. Some of the best types of homework assignments are those that help students apply what they are learning or challenge them within the range of their actual abilities and resources (Bluestein, 2012). Bluestein suggests the following:

- Keep drill work to a minimum. If doing five problems will adequately strengthen and reinforce a particular skill, why assign 20?
- Keep tabs on how your students are doing with a particular skill. To whatever degree possible, match assignments to student needs and abilities. If I cannot do long division problems in class, how successful am I likely to be doing a page of them after school?
- Be realistic about the amount of time your assignments will require. Many researchers recommend about 10 minutes per grade level per night—total! If you are not the only teacher your students have, remember that other teachers' assignments will be competing for their time.
- Offer students choices to engage their autonomy and individual learning preferences. Allow students to pick a certain number of problems on a particular page, for example, or to choose between problems on two different pages. Some students will be perfectly happy writing spelling words a certain number of times each; others will learn better by using the same words in a story or puzzle.
- Because students can indeed have a bad night, rather than relying on excuses, build some flexibility into your policy right up front. You might want to run your idea by an administrator or department chair, and ask parents to sign off as well. You will get farther with their support and parents will appreciate not having to write excuses.

Developing an environment that stresses the importance of practice is imperative, even though the homework assignment itself may not affect the grades students will see on their report cards. Classes that thrive in this framework usually have a **SUPERHERO EDUCATOR** implementing an organized plan of attack—tough to do but not impossible.

Another important piece of the organizational puzzle is the establishment of non-academic classroom procedures. Classroom rules describe acceptable and unacceptable behavior. Teachers must have a set plan for managing their classrooms—including prearranged consequences for disruptive students. Organizing and controlling this issue will make your classroom run substantially smoother.

Teachers should also have a set procedure for dealing with students who get out of their seat without permission. Having no plan for this is unacceptable! This is potentially the fastest way to lose control of your classroom. It can also be dangerous. The classes that I have observed with inadequate planning for managing students getting out of their seats were routinely encountering more physical fights compared to classrooms that utilized an organized plan.

One mistake I have seen many teachers unwittingly make happens during the distribution of supplies. Determine what procedure works best for your students and stick to it. This process should not deduct from your instructional time and should be conducted in an organized manner. If this process is not executed with integrity, it will detract from your lessons and consume teaching time. On the other hand, when done right, the time saved in the long run is incalculable. Recently, I observed a class that spent 10 minutes just passing out books. And there were only 23 children in the classroom!

Please establish clear expectations for distributing supplies. Although countless things can go wrong in the school day, passing out materials should not be one of them. I have observed classrooms that use a stopwatch to time how long it takes them to pass out books or supplies for a lesson. The goal is to be as efficient and fast as possible. The students really seemed to enjoy attempting to break the record for passing out supplies. This process helps to ensure sufficient time for instruction.

The final component of power planning that we will cover is to consider procedures for the arrival and dismissal of students. Mandate that students have some type of hall pass when leaving your room to go to the bathroom or to any other destination. The pass alerts your colleagues to the reason that your student is in the hall. It helps with acknowledging the student for good hallway behavior and assists when adults become concerned with a student being out of their classroom.

Picture in your mind the start of a school day. All of your students are in attendance. Your plans are all ready to be implemented. This will be the best day of the school year. Here are some questions I hope you considered:

- Did you imagine all the details of the morning?
- Did you envision your students entering your classroom?
- Did the students walk into your classroom and get their supplies before sitting down or did the students walk into your classroom and start working immediately?
- Do you have a morning routine established for your students to follow?

Linsin (2009) suggests several procedures to assist students entering a classroom:

- Step #1–Before asking your students to trudge outside the room and redo the procedure, wait until they're finished doing it incorrectly and are seated, quiet, and looking at you. Only then, and after a long pause, should you begin to speak.
- Step #2–Simply tell your students that they did it wrong. Don't rehash every mistake they made or remind them of how they're supposed to enter the classroom. They already know, that is, if you taught them the procedure thoroughly enough the first time.
- Step #3–In a calm voice, say, "When I say "Go" I want you to stand up, walk outside, and then come into the classroom like you are supposed to." If it is a primary classroom, you might have to walk them out yourself. However, all students benefit from following procedures with as little support from you as possible. So do not hover; watch dispassionately from a distance.
- Step #4–Do not say anything until the procedure is completed and your students are sitting and attentive.
- Step #5–If they did the "entering the classroom" procedure correctly the second time around, let them know. With a smile, say, "Now that

is how I expect you to do it every time." If, however, they did not meet your expectations, even in a small way, you need to teach it again.

Some teachers expect their students to line up before entering the classroom because they want to avoid an unsafe mad rush at the door. Right now, please decide how you want your students to enter your classroom and then remain consistent with that expectation.

Imagine that it is now the end of the school day. You have accomplished most of your learning goals. The final situation that must be addressed is dismissal. Do you dismiss your classroom by the sections in the room? Do you dismiss your classroom by boys and girls? Linsin (2012) suggests keeping your routine simple and specific and do it the same way every day. Before long it will run like a well-oiled machine; not robotic mind you, not militaristic, but a relaxed, efficient, peaceful way to end the day. The most important aspect is that you have a process for dismissal and are not allowing students the opportunity to run like cattle out of your classroom.

Debriefing Questions

1. As an educator, how organized are you?

2. Think of the best and worst teachers you have ever had; what types of organization did they demonstrate?

3. Research local companies; list two companies that excel in organization and explain what they do that is extraordinary.

4. List ten ways in which you will execute outstanding organization as a teacher.

5. Reflect on Chapter 5 Visual: If students are not organized, how can you help them?

6. Observe five different educators. Compare and contrast their organizational skills.

7. In what area are you most organized?

8. In what area are you least organized?

9. What is the connection between disorganization in the classroom and student behavior?

10. Explain how stellar organization can lead to remarkable student achievement.

Notes of Emphasis

CHAPTER 6

Base of Operations

Superhero Connection

Spiderman, with superhuman balance and agility, clings to building walls defying gravity. Spinning webs to travel effortlessly through the air chasing the bad guys, Spiderman outmaneuvers his opponent. Relying on his keen senses to detect when something is wrong, Spiderman bravely confronts the obstacle. **SUPERHERO EDUCATORS** *rely on their senses to detect classroom problems and use all of their resources to maintain an effective classroom environment.*

Impact Story

When I think of healthy school cultures, I think of all school stakeholders behaving appropriately and taking risks, while all the staff pours their personalities into their jobs. Applying this concept outside of a school environment can be tricky. I am a self-proclaimed professional people watcher. It runs in the family. I pay attention to procedures that are in place when I go to my favorite stores.

Recently, I visited store A and store B to do some onsite research. To keep the variables the same, I purchased the same two items from each store, an all-black T-shirt and a bottle of Sprite soda. When I think of a healthy organizational culture, my first focus is on management. I search for evidence that the store has an appealing purchasing environment. The specific variables I look for are the employee's behavior, appearance and helpfulness, the appearance of the store, and, finally, the behavior of the customers. Skeptics may question the part that the behavior of the customers should play, but I believe customer behavior is heavily influenced by the other variables mentioned.

I went to store A first. I immediately overheard a group of workers gossiping and other employees discussing non-related work issues. I actually heard a few who were using profanities and did not seem to care that I could overhear their conversation. All of the employees wore navy blue vests, but there was no consistent pattern of clothing after that.

I asked one employee to help me find a plain black T-shirt. She pointed in the direction of the T-shirts but did not offer any assistance beyond that. The shirts were not displayed by size and color, which meant the task of finding the one I wanted was more arduous than necessary.

Locating my Sprite was simple—outside of having to navigate around the spilled Starbucks drink on the floor. The behavior of the customers was horrific during my entire visit. I observed a customer swearing at employees, another dropping items on the floor and not picking them up, and still another who became impatient because only one checkout lane was open.

At store B, employees greeted me at the entrance and asked if I needed any assistance. All employees were wearing red T-shirts and tan pants. I asked one worker to help me find an all black T-shirt. The young man walked me straight to the rack with the plain T-shirts. Although the store had less of a selection of shirts than store A, everything was organized and easy to browse. Finding the soda was easy, and the store looked to be generally clean. The behavior of the customers was appropriate. Employee and customer interactions also appeared to be positive. Finally, store B had sufficient aisles open for customers to check out without unnecessary delay.

These two shopping experiences were totally different due to the different cultures of the two stores. Management must have a finger on the pulse of their store's "health." My experiences in store A should be concerning. The unpleasant conditions and climate could potentially influence customers to shop somewhere else. Cleanliness was an issue and products were disorganized.

Using inappropriate language is usually not inviting to customers. My customer service experience was subpar, and I will consider not shopping at store A in the future.

You might be asking, "How does this relate to a school's culture?" Well, I am aware of many parents who choose schools largely based on the culture. The same variables come into play: behavior of the employees (the way teachers carry themselves), appearance of the employees (how the teachers are dressed), helpfulness of the employees (teaching ability), appearance of the store (cleanliness of the classroom and school building) and behavior of the customers (the students).

Innovative Connections

When I visualize an organization that embodies a rich and strong culture, I think of the Entertainment Sports and Programming Network (ESPN). In 1978, faced with unemployment after being fired from his job as Communications Director for the New England Whalers (now the Carolina Hurricanes), Bill Rasmussen founded ESPN with his son, Scott Rasmussen ("How it Started," 2017). Entrepreneurial daring, irrepressible enthusiasm and a dash of good luck soon gave America its first 24-hour sports network.

Once unleashed upon sports fans, ESPN's impact forever changed the way we watch television. ESPN is considered the leader in sports programming and dominates cable television, radio sports talk, and Internet sports reporting. ESPN's cable channels collect more than $5 a month from each of the nearly 100 million American households that subscribe to pay TV, more than any other channel by far. That comes to about $6.5 billion in revenue, without even considering advertising. With an estimated value between $40 billion and $60 billion, ESPN is at least 20 times bigger than the New York Times Company, or five times bigger than News Corp. (Thompson, 2013).

The culture of ESPN allows employees to be themselves. Most on-air personalities do not fit the mold of the typical news broadcaster. A majority of their broadcasters are very relatable and very much like the common man. Their hosts use slang, improper English and poke fun at the athletes. This is considerably different from what is seen on most local news markets. In order for the on-air talents on ESPN to flourish, there must be a culture of shared leadership and the ability to be creative in their working environment. ESPN is a case in point that shows how executives can sponsor leadership in its employees by having a supportive culture and allowing its employees the flexibility to be creative (Hargreaves & Fink, 2007).

Please close your eyes and take a minute to reflect upon the organizational culture of your "base of operations." How close is your organization to being recognized as great? Pay attention to your work culture. Does the culture allow you to be great or does it stop you from being great? Success starts with you. When you go to work tomorrow, walk in and be great. You are a **SUPERHERO EDUCATOR!**

Education Research and Focus

When students do not achieve at expected levels, very few teachers will step up and accept responsibility. The teacher will place fault on students, parents, or poverty as reason explaining why students can't learn (Gollnick & Chinn, 2017). High performing schools, however, overcome this attitude by developing a positive culture for all school stakeholders. We call this the "All Star Five" for effective school culture. The "All Star Five" culture consists of five elements: Vision, Collaboration, Customer Service, Community, and Desire. Some schools, unfortunately, may accomplish only one of the "All Star Five" elements, while others max out at three or four. It is a rare honor to reach and maintain all of the components that construct an "All Star Five" school culture.

The first element is vision—the ability to fully grasp what desired outcomes look like, understand how to get stakeholders to align their actions to the desired outcomes, and the ability to see success before it actually happens. Koppelman (2017) found teacher's attitudes to be a main factor in student learning. Successful teachers exhibit a positive attitude. Establishing an organizational culture that supports a positive learning environment is essential.

Ms. Boston was the new principal at Martin Luther King Middle School (MLK), replacing a principal that had worked there for several years. The school's academic achievement was average, which signals that at least they were doing something right. The morale of the school staff, however, was uneven. If a teacher was on the past principal's good side, he or she felt positive about the school. If a teacher was on the principal's bad side, that teacher was discontented. The previous principal had a history of embarrassing people in staff meetings and did not support certain teachers when dealing with parents. Professional growth opportunities were nearly non-existent.

Ms. Boston knew from the beginning that she needed **SUPERHERO EDUCATORS** to transform an average learning environment into a highly effective one. The first thing Ms. Boston did was to take a personal interest in each staff member. She learned what made each staff member tick, which allowed her to find common ground based on personal interests. This positive approach quickly spread to teachers, who began to interact differently with colleagues, students and parents. Because of this change in attitude, the staff at Martin Luther King could begin to address various barriers to improved performance. The school climate strengthened because Ms. Boston intentionally sought to secure a healthy work environment.

Ms. Carey thrived in this positive environment, finally feeling valued. In her new role as the Health and Wellness Champion—a position formerly held only by favorites of the old principal—she asked both the staff and parents to complete a survey during the first week of school to assess what health and wellness initiatives worked well the previous year and what needed significant improvement. Both staff and parents ranked improving parental relationships as the number one area in need of a boost. Armed with this knowledge, Ms. Carey developed a new vision that transformed the culture of the school to one that supported the important relationship between parents and teachers.

The second element of the "All Star Five" is collaboration. Understanding that a collaborative partnership with families would positively impact academic outcomes, Ms. Boston needed someone to model how to effectively interact with parents and turned to one of the school's most established—and most frustrated—teachers, Mr. Wiggins. In spite of his experience and understanding of how a school should be run, he had become increasingly frustrated under the previous principal. But now, with the support of Ms. Boston, he could act on his belief that when a school meets the needs of families, the credibility of the school as a whole increases. Mr. Wiggins was a natural at collaborating with parents and understood how families must help meet the needs of students. He knew that without a strong parent-teacher relationship, a school simply cannot meet the needs of students (Gallavan, 2011).

Mr. Wiggins began modeling the following behaviors: greeting parents at the door when available, participating in afterschool events regardless of whether or not he was being paid, calling home for more positive than negative phone calls, injecting humor when interacting with parents, talking sports with parents, being honest with parents, and having the unique ability to calm parents when they were obviously irritated. Mr. Wiggins' positive attitude quickly caught on, transforming the school's relationship with parents. Because of all this, he has become known as the unofficial school Dad. We prefer donning Mr. Wiggins the title of **SUPERHERO EDUCATOR**.

The third factor of the "All Star Five" to assess is Customer Service. Like Mr. Wiggins, Ms. Davis had been frustrated with the previous administration. But under the leadership of Ms. Boston, she became one of the most energetic individuals in the entire building at MLK. Now, she rarely complains about a bad day. More importantly, she honestly loves her job. It is practically impossible to surpass her work ethic. Plus, she delights in seeing the impact this hard work has on her students. Ms. Davis lives to serve. Her customer service efforts are most evident when she mediates issues with parents before needing to involve Ms. Boston. Overall, parents have come to trust that the school has everyone's best interest at heart.

The fourth component of a healthy school culture is Community. The days of schools working in isolation are long gone. Schools are expected to open the door for community involvement. The expectation has become that local communities will connect with their neighborhood schools in some way. This can be slightly awkward because neither side really knows how to interact with the other. It takes a **SUPERHERO EDUCATOR** to get the ball rolling.

Ms. Barnes was a naturally shy teacher. Ms. Boston was initially unsure what to think of her. Ms. Boston challenged her staff to build strategic partnerships with the community. Ms. Barnes was quick to offer several plans, potentially benefiting both the school and several local organizations. Within one month, she had lined up four potential organizations to partner with donating their time and resources to the students. This has developed into a significant partnership that has been advantageous to the school community in many ways. Students are allowed to job shadow in the community several times a year. The community now provides financial support for important events and even supports professional development for faculty and staff.

The fifth and final element is Desire, and the new principal found her champion in Ms. Jefferies, a 3rd grade teacher in her second year of teaching. Although veteran educators had ridiculed her for her innovative ways of teaching and challenging her students, she understood the importance of developing positive relationships with her students (Ladson-Billings, 2009). The veteran teachers, on the other hand, resented how effective she was with her students. Ms. Jefferies' desire to be great remained unaltered. The ridicule actually increased her motivation to be a **SUPERHERO EDUCATOR.**

Ms. Boston quickly recognized Ms. Jefferies' talent and passion and began actively supporting her efforts. Even though Ms. Jefferies had a better grasp of the language arts curriculum than most of the veteran teachers, she still had a desire to progress. She took her class on a field trip once a month, always including her special education students. Ms. Jefferies did not want any of her students to be deprived of opportunities to grow.

Ms. Jefferies was adamant that all of her students participate in every aspect of the school environment, not just the learning experiences in her classroom. Her students volunteered as peer mentors, picked up trash regularly, read morning announcements, were reading buddies to the younger students, and had their best projects displayed throughout the school building. Ms. Jefferies students were comfortable with being showcased and proud of the contributions they made to enhance their school environment. Her desire to be a great educator has led her students to have many meaningful experiences both inside and outside the classroom.

It is vital that your school culture is healthy and vibrant. The classroom environment dictates how students behave and achieve. The "All Star 5" is the ultimate formula for addressing these objectives. **SUPERHERO EDUCATORS** consider their base of operations as having utmost relevance.

Debriefing Questions

1. Which of the "All Star Five" is easiest for you to achieve? Explain your response.

2. Which of the "All Star Five" is hardest for you to achieve? Explain your response.

3. At your school environment, which of the "All Star Five" exist?

4. Would your students, staff, and parents describe your school environment differently than your response to question number 3?

5. Reflect on Chapter 6 Visual: When dreaming of your organized classroom, what are the real life barriers?

6. Reflect upon field trips you have taken: How was planning done to ensure that all students could participate?

7. Describe the staff member that best illustrates working under a customer service framework.

8. What are three examples of your school collaborating with the local community?
If there are no community partnerships, list three possible examples.

9. How would your peers rate your classroom environment?

10. Does your work environment and student academic results match? Explain your response.

Notes of Emphasis

CHAPTER 7

Sphere of Service

Superhero Connection

I am Iron Man. Armor, jet boots, pulse beams, and missile launchers. I am Iron Man. Lasers, tasers, and flamethrowers. I am Iron Man. Iron Man saves villagers and destroys terrorists, all while battling issues with his arc reactor. These health problems are not an excuse for poor performance. Iron Man suppresses his personal problems and aggressively pursues his targets of evil. How do we pursue our goals when challenged with different obstacles?

Impact Story

"One, two, three, four...." I was silently counting to ten in an effort to calm myself. I had wanted to quickly order a hot sandwich and then hop back into my car for the long ride home. No one had taken my order: in fact, no one had come to the front counter to even acknowledge my presence as I waited for what felt like an eternity. I noticed one worker using a mop as an imaginary sword to battle the tables he was attempting to clean. Behind the counter there were two workers wrestling with each other for position, a battle to get to a food item first. Upon closer observation, it was clear that the tussling was just an excuse to flirt with each other in an awkward way. Any attempt to get their attention was futile. The attraction was just way too strong.

The only other employee that I could see was back in the kitchen, frantically cooking the burgers, chicken, and other sandwiches. No acknowledgement was given to me, my time at the counter, or my repetitive coughing and throat clearing. Finally, I yelled out, "Could someone please take my order?" The young man leading the mop into battle responded, "Just a minute, bro, I am winning the ultimate quest." I flashed a fake smile and walked out of there as fast as I could. As I drove out of the parking lot with an empty stomach, I wondered if those bizarre images of such awful customer service would ever be forgotten. I guess not.

Innovative Connections

Great teachers excel in customer service. This service is intentional in its scope and purpose. Retail giant Amazon ranks in the top 100 of globally known brands across seven major industries for best customer service (Allen, 2012). With over 200 million customers, Amazon has mastered the customer-centered approach. If you build a great experience, customers tell each other, and the company's culture becomes pervasive (Archer, 2015). Every worker at Amazon is required to spend time working the customer service phone line. By requiring these efforts, Amazon is putting the customer at the center of all its interactions, a constant reminder when decisions are made at higher levels in the company structure. The mission of Amazon is simple: "Be the 'Best' in delivering service. Improve the lives and businesses with those whom we connect. Serve others the way we want to be served" (Marques, 2014).

Other companies well known for customer service include Starbucks, Nordstrom, Chick-fil-A, and Marriot. Regardless of the business, the quality of an organization's treatment of its customers is a key to success.

Education Research and Focus

"Good morning! How are you?" I greet my students outside of my classroom, welcoming the children every morning. This daily routine offers students a consistent invitation to join in on the fun. Yes, learning is enjoyable! The classroom is the place to be and each child is gladly expected to be part of this excitement. The stage is now set for learning and, through this ritual, I grab a glimpse at possible problematic behaviors. Take Malcolm, for example, who talked back to his mom when she questioned why he needs to listen to Ariana Grande songs while doing his homework. Due to Malcolm's angry response, his mother took his cell phone away. The next day, when I greet Malcolm at the classroom door and shake his hand, he gloomily gazes to the floor and mumbles a greeting. The response is a red flag, and I talk to Malcolm privately about what is wrong. Without this early detection, his whole day of learning may be in jeopardy.

In my teaching training courses, I recall instructors advising us not to smile until Thanksgiving. The idea was that students need to take us seriously and they will not if we smile. But we know that this will not work with today's students. Great customer service demands high student engagement. Learning can be extremely hard work and must be surrounded and supported by a positive environment filled with approval, playful interactions, and personal storytelling. Remember that this classroom environment must be highly structured, clean, and bright.

A teacher who masters strong customer service invites parents and guardians to be a part of the learning process. I caution you not to set arbitrary guidelines for parents to observe their own son or daughter in your class, such as requiring a 24-48 hours advance notice of their visit. This unnecessarily raises suspicion and doubt with parents. Instead the message needs to be: "Please come and see your child doing great work anytime you wish. Parents, you are always invited and encouraged to assist in the classroom, sign up to lead events, or drop off donated items on the class wish list." A true partnership in learning is then fostered.

When Kamisa goes home and says that her teacher yells at her and does not let her ask questions in social studies class, the parent quickly cries foul. Witnessing the teacher's actions and behaviors reduces the parental concerns and alternately fosters a solid teacher advocate. Every teacher generates and develops a reputation. What is your reputation as an educator? You should work hard to create a constructive reputation with your school's stakeholders. If you do not intentionally set out to create your reputation, someone will fill in the blanks for you. Parents talk outside of the classroom, in the school hallways, and in the parking lots. Let them rave about how wonderful you are with their child, not rant about how you fail to communicate or how you struggle with classroom management, or how overwhelmed you seem.

When parents drop off their most important person in the world for seven hours a day, they should have very high expectations. In fact, **SUPERHERO EDUCATORS** thrive in an environment of high expectations, often surpassing those of average teachers. Let students know what they are achieving and communicate to parents the effects of your teaching. Your administrators must also be alerted to all that is being accomplished in your classroom. Build awareness in the community by highlighting what students are able to do in your classroom because of your teaching. Seek funding to take your teaching to the next level. This is your reputation. This is exceptional customer service. The community will be overjoyed with its investment in the local school and wants more of you.

Mark Sanborn (2008) details the importance of building relationships in a technology-driven society where relationships are in danger of becoming a lost art. His seven principles on improving relationships are noteworthy. Be real, be interested, be a better listener, be empathic, be honest, be helpful, and be prompt. These simple principles create loyalty and are the basis of partnerships and teamwork.

A popular saying highlights the importance of building authentic relationships: "Students will not respect you until you respect them." Some educators bristle at this statement, thinking that they do not aim to be a student's friend or buddy. True, sharing pictures with students on social media or communicating about your weekends' activities is not appropriate. Respecting your students by showing they are valued and loved, however, is essential.

Famous Dave's is a fabulous place for ribs and barbequed chicken. Dave Anderson, the founder of Famous Dave's, shares his inside secret to success. Develop a personal and powerhouse introduction. When asked how he is doing, Dave may reply, "I am better than ever! I am rockin' and rollin', hunky dory, feeling groovy, settin' the world on fire, got a tiger by the tail, if I felt any better they would have to call the pOOleece!" (Anderson & Anderson, 2010). Dave's unique delivery separates him from his counterparts and makes the receiver of his passionate responses feel inspired.

Attending your students' events, games, recitals, and other activities demonstrates a strong commitment to them. This means you care about your students' lives. It demonstrates that teaching is more than a job for you. When I taught in middle school, I asked students to bring in a schedule of the events they would like me to go watch. I posted these events on a bulletin board. Throughout the week, I would hit a few events—depending on my schedule. Upon first glance at that board, it seemed impossibly overwhelming with the dozens of schedules stapled there. Yet as you strategically plan, you will discover that it is possible and the effort is definitely worth it.

One day, for example, I might get to an after school basketball game. When I enter the gym, I quickly greet as many parents as I can. My presence lets parents know I care about their child and offers them a different perspective on my personality. After 15 minutes of watching the game and making sure my students see me, I would get up and leave. On my way home, I might stop by the dance studio to see two of my students practice their dance routine. I touch base with the parents, make sure my two students see me, and then I leave after about 15 minutes. This extra 30 minutes of my time was enjoyable and also promoted a strong rapport with my school's families. The next day, students talk proudly about my attendance at their events and I can discuss the event to motivate students. Parents will support me and give me extra backing because of these positive interactions.

Parents are partners in the educational journey with teachers. Frustrated parents may think that teachers are not doing the best they can or may even deem them ineffective. Frustrated teachers view parents as obstacles who do not understand teaching or education in general. The truth is that teachers are assisting parents in educating their children. Parents are the primary educators. Teachers have the awesome privilege of assisting parents in this important task.

The collaboration between parent and teacher begins with the teacher's willingness to listen and learn from parents. When parents hear affirmation from the teacher that they are needed and essential, they respond positively. As experts in customer service, teachers communicate with parents regularly through electronic newsletters, emails, face to face contact, a website, or phone calls. **SUPERHERO EDUCATORS** know when to communicate, how to deliver the message, and what format works best.

Do not place a limit on communication with parents. Email is a common form of communicating with parents that most teachers use, but be aware of the danger that comes from this relatively impersonal medium. When possible, communicate in the most direct format, which is face to face. When time and other constraints make this impossible, use video conferencing or a phone call. If all else fails try email or a note home. This hierarchy needs to be followed even when parents may use email as their primary form of communication.

A common mistake in parent and teacher communication is exemplified in the following scenario. After school one day, Ollie gets home from school and sits down to study. Ollie's mom asks what he is studying. Ollie explains that there is a math test tomorrow and that he could use some help understanding two major concepts. Ollie's mom does not know how to solve these math problems and asks how the teacher explained the concepts. With great drama, Ollie describes how the teacher abruptly dismissed his questions while disciplining two other students. Tears begin flowing down Ollie's cheeks.

Immediately, his mother logs onto her computer and angrily types a strongly worded email to the teacher. The message explains that Ollie was studying diligently for the upcoming math test but because specific concepts were left untaught, her son should not be penalized on those questions. Ollie's mom indicates she will be talking to the school principal to see why student behaviors are adversely affecting learning in the classroom.

SUPERHERO EDUCATORS know that the proper reply should be a simple message, such as, "Thank you for your communication. Let's talk about this in person. I am available any time this evening or tomorrow. Please let me know what works for you." This ability to take a deep breath, understand the limitations of email and not rush to respond is an enormous blessing. Miscommunication is to be expected when working with people. Remember, you are the professional educator and parents are your customers with a right to a high quality product—your superior teaching.

The above example illustrates the complexity of teaching. Every job has its ups and downs, but teaching is exceptionally personal and deals with many different dynamics. There are days that go extremely well and you realize the tremendous impact you are having, but then a day comes along that makes you question why you have chosen this profession. Knowing these extreme highs and extreme lows will be a real part of your teaching journey, you must prepare through anticipation. Acknowledge that your days will consist of highs and lows throughout your school year. Develop a plan of attack to tackle the emotions and feelings of the discouraging days. On a very bad day, you may need to set aside time for coffee with a friend who helps you keep everything in perspective. On a very good day, you may want to reach out to family members to share what worked. Knowing these ups and downs exist in teaching, you must strive to be consistent. Being consistently positive is truly difficult work, but a necessity.

Students should never know when you are having a bad day. Your car did not start that morning, you misplaced your credit card, your girlfriend broke up with you, and someone broke into your apartment are not excuses. You must still be a joyful, patient and caring teacher in the classroom. Pretend you are happy even if you do not actually feel it. Yes, fake it. Students come every day to your class to experience educational greatness. But shouldn't you warn the students that today is not the day to misbehave? No! Model how you handle adversity and problem solve without losing patience. Students need to be able to depend upon a consistently positive educator. Humor works well during tough situations. Through humor, teachers can stay focused on the student's well-being and maintain a positive classroom environment. **SUPERHERO EDUCATORS** acknowledge unexpected barriers in their lives but always teach at a high level, even modeling being positive during adverse times.

Although a hobby or interest outside of teaching can assist with keeping a positive attitude, be careful that your hobby does not begin to take precedent over teaching. Teachers that coach basketball may spend hours planning practices, designing drills, developing game strategy, and reviewing game film. This passion for coaching is fantastic, but the same amount of time and energy, or more, needs to be put into your classroom. Teaching is your full time job; coaching is a hobby. Let students, teachers, administrators, and community members see your passion for teaching. Spend hours planning your lessons, practicing innovative teaching methods, developing new ways of communicating, and reviewing student data.

Teaching is one of the most rewarding professions in the world. Demonstrate this through your positive words and actions. Once you become effective at customer service, you will be better positioned to positively influence student achievement, the true charge of **SUPERHERO EDUCATORS.**

Debriefing Questions

1. As an educator, who are your customers?

2. How do you manage unexpected circumstances outside of school so that they do not affect your high quality teaching?

3. Research local companies, list the top five companies that excel in customer service and explain what they do that is extraordinary.

4. List ten ways in which you will display outstanding customer service as a teacher.

5. Reflect on Chapter 7 Visual: Which frame describes your past experiences in school? Explain the positives and negatives.

6. Observe five different educators. Record and evaluate how each teacher displays strong customer service.

7. From the chapter, select three successful businesses. As a teacher, what customer service strategies did you identify that you can employ at your school?

8. Reflect on your individual gifts, how can these strengths further develop excellent customer service?

9. How do you balance the vast responsibilities of teaching and your outside hobbies?

10. Explain how stellar customer service can lead to remarkable student achievement.

Notes of Emphasis

CHAPTER 8
Dedicated to Diversity

Superhero Connection

The Incredibles are an unusual family. Every family member has individual superhero powers. The Incredibles live their lives concealing their powers. It is dramatic to watch their transition from a normal family to superheroes. During the day they are the Parr family, but at a time of need they become the Incredibles. In the end, the family learns to embrace their dualistic lifestyle. Their strength is in their diversity. With each member of the family possessing a different superpower, they conquer the enemy by utilizing one another's strengths. **SUPERHERO EDUCATORS** *recognize diversity in their students as a strength.*

Impact Story

As we watch our favorite television show, movie, or even advertisement, we are often struck by how good looking the actors and models are. Obviously, producers intentionally utilize extremely attractive people to sell products while enhancing our viewing pleasure. This meets our expectations and satisfies our senses. The problem with this normalizing of almost flawless beauty is that we consequently may perceive ourselves as not all that attractive. We notice countless flaws and play a dangerous game with shaming our self-image.

In the early 2000s, Dove executives began looking for a way to breathe life into a brand that was being overshadowed by other companies. As a consequence, Dove attempted to redefined beauty through its "Real Beauty" campaign, which promoted the beauty of natural variations in female body shapes and sizes. The audience for Dove products expanded dramatically.

Like commercials, television has something for everyone. Cable channels air shows that fit into practically every cultural demographic. Although underrepresentation of some groups certainly does exist, there is a show on television for most demographics. If you want to watch a black sitcom, there is Black Entertainment Television (BET). If you want to watch shows from a female perspective the Lifetime Channel could be of interest. If you are into animals, there is Animal Planet TV. If you are into sports or politics, there are numerous channels. To my surprise some people actually watch the Weather Channel most of the time. The point is there is so much diversity on television that everyone has a chance to be satisfied.

Innovative Connections

Diversity has become an increasingly important issue in America at large and in politics in general. As of the writing of this book, only four states—California, New Mexico, Texas and Hawaii—are what are called majority minority states, that is, states in which the majority of the population are members of one or more minority group. The projections are that approximately 22 states—two-thirds of the country's population—will be majority minority states in a few years. ("As diversity increases," 2017). The minority population will have risen to 56 percent of the total population as compared to 38 percent as of 2014 (Wazwaz, 2015).

As a result of this increased diverse population, issues of the role of minorities in the United States has become increasingly front and center. During both the Democratic and Republican national conventions, both political parties promoted diversity—perhaps more during this election than ever before. Both parties showcased everyone from African Americans, Asians, and Caucasians to coal miners, teachers and veterans. Both political parties desperately attempted to focus on embracing diversity. In fact, both parties claimed to be the leader in celebrating diversity.

As is so often the case, the rest of the country is far ahead of its politicians in the matter of diversity, no more so than in the area of professional sports. Although most are becoming increasingly diverse, the National Basketball Association (NBA) has traditionally stood out from the other professional franchises. According to a "report by the Institute for Diversity and Ethics in Sport, the NBA received an A-plus grade for racial hiring and B-plus for gender hiring on its annual report card. Its overall grade of A was its seventh in a row. For the second straight year, more than 35 percent of all professional employees within the NBA league office were people of color, and 40 percent were women. There were also 45 women employed at the vice president level or higher. Four women also served as presidents or CEOs of NBA teams, the highest total among men's professional sports leagues (Study, 2014).

Educational Research and Focus

You must embrace and accept diversity. More than that, you have a responsibility to do so. Researchers have documented that students' exposure to other students who are different from themselves and the novel ideas and challenges that such exposure brings leads to improved cognitive skills, including critical thinking and problem solving (Wells, Fox, & Cordova-Cobo, 2016). Although some teachers are afraid of diversity and do not consider diversity in their classroom as a good thing, we must get over the fear! Diverse students are already in your classrooms. Why would having diversity in your classroom not be a good thing?

Dealing competently with cultural diversity requires a certain knowledge base. First, you must believe that cultural diversity is a good thing. When a teacher does not embrace diversity, impenetrable barriers will appear. Teachers who do not embrace diversity will negatively impact the success of their students (Genishi & Dyson, 2009). As an educator, you must know how your school confronts the needs of diverse learners. A proactive approach will help generate "wins" as it pertains to cultural diversity. Celebrating diversity in your class will lead to so many teachable moments. Most importantly, embracing diversity will allow you to foster magical working relationships with your students and enable you to meet their academic needs.

One of the most important ways of embracing diversity is to make a genuine effort to understand and support the uniqueness of each of your students. Consider the following (Souto-Manning & Martell, 2017):

- Make it a habit to identify every child's potential.
- Commit to learning about and from your students, their families, and communities.
- Listen to your students—especially during more unstructured times (choice time, play, and mealtime) when they are more likely to engage in authentic discussions.
- Engage students in developing critical consciousness.

Some educators live outside of the communities where they teach, which tends to prevent them from being culturally relevant. Even if you do not live in the community of your school, the respect you will gain by learning about the community you serve will be invaluable for your students. This process was my greatest secret weapon as a new teacher. I attended local church services, community receptions, sporting events, and musical recitals. I particularly used this strategy on my worst behaved students. It worked like a charm every single time. After attending several of their events, the behaviorally challenged students were far less likely to act out in my classroom.

Engaging parents is an important way of embracing cultural diversity. Parental involvement is critical for ensuring academic growth. Academic growth is more likely when the classroom culture recognizes diversity as a strength. Effective collaboration between parents and teachers is imperative (Minkle, Sheridan, Kim, Ryoo, & Koziol, 2014). At times this can pose challenges. When calling a student's home or during parent conferences, please make sure you correctly pronounce the names of the students. Assigning nicknames because we fumble with a student's name is unacceptable and only communicates that we do not really care about our students as unique individuals. A failure like this can taint the views of parents when we call home with a concern.

I had a parent tell me during my first year of teaching to stop calling about a behavior concern until I learned how to properly say her daughter's name. Although I was initially upset with that conversation, after some reflection, I conceded that the parent was absolutely correct. I was not embracing the cultural diversity of my classroom. If I can remember how to accurately pronounce the name of Larshamaka, you can too.

Pronouncing names is one important, crucial step for embracing cultural diversity in the classroom. Teachers must realize that regardless of their benign intentions, students may see them as part of the dominant school structure that many students resist. Once teachers adjust their awareness, they will see the cultural diversity as a powerful aid to learning. Teachers must turn theory into practice, embracing students' cultural capital through innovative pedagogic methods to better engage them in the classroom (Goldenberg, 2013).

Learn about and create a diversity calendar. Encourage students to identify all holidays, birthdays and cultural events, which will enhance student and family engagement under the umbrella of cultural diversity. Can you imagine how powerful this could be for students who may not yet have been exposed to traditions from other cultures? Can you imagine all of the teachable moments for an educator? By celebrating diversity, your students will become more aware of cultures other than their own—certainly one of the goals of education. Milner (2010) states when teachers rely on their dominant culture, they can lose student engagement because of cultural barriers. White teachers in particular must recognize their cultural differences and learn to embrace the cultures of their students.

Another step in a positive direction would be to host a cultural connection fair. This could take the form of a large school-wide event or a smaller project for your classroom. Take the lead and show off the diversity that you enjoy within your classroom. Planning for an event like this might begin with deciding what aspects of the culture you want to showcase—food, music, history, clothing or art. If you feel disconcerted about where to start, ask your students. I find that often students show far more creativity and outside-of-the-box thinking than adults, especially when it comes to sharing their own cultures. Students typically expel more effort in this kind of relevant activity than in completing the odd numbers on a math homework sheet.

SUPERHERO EDUCATORS have the unique ability to infuse culture into classwork and homework. Embedding cultural awareness into your teaching is one of the quickest ways to develop and ensure student engagement. If you feel as though you do not have a good handle on the backgrounds of the students you serve, watch the social relations and communication patterns that take place between parents and students. This will often offer strategic insights.

Brown Port K-8 School in Milwaukee, has a more diverse student population than other schools in its district, and Mr. Taylor, an 8th grade teacher, believes that the cultures of his students are beneficial in meeting the academic and behavioral needs of his students. At the beginning of each year, he takes a cultural inventory to learn about each of his student's backgrounds. He uncovers a great deal about the different cultures found in his classroom. He finds that some students did not even recognize that they have a culture. Early in the school year, each student is required to bring in a cultural artifact from home that reflects his or her culture. This process serves as a learning opportunity for all students and establishes a level of acceptance for all cultures. Through discussion, his students often learn that they have more in common with other cultures than they had originally thought.

During the holiday season, grandparents are invited to Mr. Taylor's classroom to speak words of encouragement and share stories of what school was like for them in their childhoods. This proves to be very powerful for all. Most students do not realize the struggles their grandparents had to endure just to make it to school. The grandparents plead with the kids to do their best and take advantage of their opportunities in school, which leaves a valuable impression on the students. Mr. Taylor often preaches the same message, but it truly hits home coming from their grandparents' lips.

Mr. Taylor is a **SUPERHERO EDUCATOR** because he figured out two essentials for great teaching. First, students love to share their cultures. These opportunities provide an extremely high level of student engagement. Students want their classmates to understand their home lives. Indirectly, these opportunities also invoke the most parental support. Parents are willing to do whatever is necessary to help their child share cultural examples with the classroom.

Second, Mr. Taylor's entire class benefits from celebrating cultural diversity. Mr. Taylor's class has the fewest behavior incident referrals documented in the school office. I strongly believe this occurs because students genuinely respect each other so they are less likely to degrade their peers. His students generally get along and learn the art of accepting differences, an important quality in an increasingly diverse America.

The most profound benefit to emerge as a result of his teaching is the leadership displayed by Mr. Taylor's students. With his guidance, the students take their cultural show on the road. The class visits all the younger grade level classrooms presenting what they learned from each other. This instantly develops a model for leadership, as the younger students idolized Mr. Taylor's students. Mr. Taylor deserves the credit for being a **SUPERHERO EDUCATOR** who embraces diversity and harnesses the power that lies within its variance.

Debriefing Questions

1. As an educator, how is diversity embraced in your classroom?

2. List twenty ways in which we are diverse (visible and invisible).

3. Research local companies; list five companies that excel in cultural diversity and explain what they do that is extraordinary.

4. List ten additional ways in which you will embrace cultural diversity as a teacher.

5. Reflect on the Chapter 8 Visual: Summarize this chart in one sentence.

6. Observe five different educators. Record and evaluate how each teacher embraces diversity.

7. Reflect upon a teacher that does not celebrate diversity. Is the classroom successful?

8. Reflect on your individual gifts; how can these strengths be used to further embrace diversity?

9. Explain how embracing diversity is easy/difficult for you

10. Explain how embracing of diversity can lead to remarkable student achievement.

Notes of Emphasis

CHAPTER 9

Cosmic Collaboration

Superhero Connection

Researching the cartoon series "The Super Friends" brought back wonderful childhood memories. Aquaman, Batman, Robin, Superman, Wonder Woman, The Atom, Firestorm, The Flash, Green Lantern, Hawkgirl, Hawkman, and The Wonder Twins are the heroes that comprise the team of Super Friends. Each of these characters possessed a unique superpower, and working collectively they vanquished the villains and helped each other succeed. They were powerful with their individual strengths, but when they joined forces they became unbeatable. Do you have super friends that you frequently collaborate with to gain incredible achievements?

Impact Story

Several years ago I had surgery on my throat. I had a medical intravenous injection (IV) inserted into my left arm. Medicine, as was standard procedure, was administered to sedate me during the surgical process. After the IV was in place, I felt myself becoming tired. It was just a matter of time before the medication would take over and I would fall into a deep sleep.

Suddenly, something changed. A severe pain radiated through my left arm. I have experienced an IV before, but this sensation was completely new. My arm started turning blue. My first thought was, "I am going to die right here in the pre-op." The pain and blue color in my left arm worsened. I began pinching myself to try to fight the sleepiness that was taking over. In my mind, time was slipping away. Unable to speak, my last ditch effort to stop this train wreck was to flail my other arm in an attempt to get the attention of the nurse. She immediately removed the device that was lodged in my mouth, and I quickly explained the pain in my arm.

When she looked at my arm and saw it was turning blue, she removed the IV immediately. I overheard a different nurse mutter in disgust, "She messed up another simple IV." Another nurse made a comment that "she" should not be allowed to put an IV in anyone's arm. I was thankful when they removed the IV, as the pain subsided, but I was still scared to death of what could have happened if it had gone unchecked.

A group of nurses stayed in the room with me the remaining time, but the nurse who botched the IV did not return. This was the first outward evidence of the nursing staff collaborating with one another, although it occurred as the result of the original nurse's mistake. It put me at ease knowing that multiple nurses were overseeing my care. They kept me informed each step of the way, which included bringing a hospital specialist in to administer a new IV for me and informing me of the doctor's expected arrival time. There is a good chance I would have requested postponing the surgery if I had not seen the nurses collaborating so effectively. Too bad the struggling nurse did not seek out nor was offered assistance. When a staff works together, avoiding and solving problems becomes much easier. Reflect on your work place environment. When was the last time you collaborated with a coworker?

Innovative Connections

Working in the airline industry is a demanding profession, and every worker in the industry plays an important role in ensuring safe and efficient travel. The U.S. Department of Transportation's Bureau of Transportation Statistics reported U.S. airlines and foreign airlines serving the United States carried an all-time high of 895.5 million system wide (domestic and international) scheduled service passengers in 2015, 5.0 percent more than the previous record high of 853.1 million reached in 2014 (Smallen, 2016).

Those numbers emphasize the importance of every employee in the airline industry, and each piece of the employee puzzle must be in place for your flight experience to be successful. Although there are specific roles for employees, their collaboration is imperative for the success of an airline. Clearly defined roles in the airline industry allow each individual to become proficient at what they do. When it is time to collaborate, each person brings his or her expertise to the table.

One frustrating and stressful situation that can inconvenience both the passengers and the employees is the loss of luggage. According to Southan (2016) more than 23 million suitcases were mishandled during their journey through the world's airports. In their attempts to locate the missing luggage, airline representatives are forced to collaborate with each other. Think of all the conversations that must take place between the customer, the airline check-in staff, the baggage handlers, and the customer service departments.

I have experienced airline collaboration on multiple levels. Several years ago, my family took a trip to Orlando, Florida. After landing at Orlando International, my family could not wait to embark upon the Disney adventures we had planned. The schedule was tightly packed on that first day. Time was of the essence. If we missed any event, we would be out of luck because of a no refund policy.

The first order of business was picking up our luggage. We waited patiently as we watched other people anxiously grab their bags off the carousel. My wife and kids soon came across their suitcases, while I continued to wait patiently for mine. As the baggage claim area emptied, it became apparent that we had a problem—my baggage had not surfaced.

I hurried to customer service while my family waited in the baggage claim area on the off chance that my suitcase might magically appear. The representative at customer service contacted two different people to search for my luggage. After communicating with several departments, the lost suitcase was found. But time was quickly running out, and it looked as if we might miss our transportation to the hotel. Customer service, however, saved the day by calling our transport bus and requesting it wait for us. Rather quickly, the ordeal was over, and we could now enjoy the Happiest Place on Earth.

I have always remembered this experience as a great example of cooperation. One person alone would never have been able to track down the luggage, transport it to my location and help my family board our bus on time. The airline staff had to collaborate efficiently to solve this problem.

Educational Research and Focus

Effective collaboration for a **SUPERHERO EDUCATOR** is best highlighted by analyzing an educator who takes an opposite, solitary approach to teaching. Let's call her Ms. Miller. Teaching in the second grade for 20 years, Ms. Miller would commonly be described as a "know it all." Collaborating with peers is unnecessary from her point of view. The desks in her classroom must stand in straight rows. She is convinced this is the best method to maintain law and order in the classroom. She only calls a student's home to address a behavior problem. Even if one of her student's is not meeting academic expectations, no phone call is made. Her lesson plans are detailed but are sadly the same lesson plans she has used for the last 15 years. She rejects the fact that technology, research, student behavior, and assessment tools have all changed since she entered the field of education.

Ms. Miller is self-isolated. She purposefully lives on her own little island. Her motto is, "I teach my class. You teach your class. Don't bother me and I won't bother you." Her students' test scores have flatlined the last four years. Perceptive parents have noticed the patterns in her behavior and many have asked that their kids be assigned to a different teacher. And of course, Ms. Miller does not collaborate with school administration, consistently rejecting her principal's help and flatly ignoring opportunities for professional development and networking. Everyone knows of the problems in her cloistered classroom. Ms. Miller insists that everyone else is the problem. Her peers believe that she is simply terrified to have her weaknesses exposed.

Now in contrast to the isolation of Ms. Miller let's take a look at the expert collaboration of Ms. Riley, a highly effective special education teacher, a **SUPERHERO EDUCATOR** born to work with others.

We call the following steps for executing effective collaborative efforts for improvement the "Supportive 7." Let's see how Ms. Riley embodies this supportive process:

Step 1–Develop collaborative vision/goals for the school, departments, and content area teams.

Many educators call this a school improvement plan, and Ms. Riley applied such a plan to the special education department. Schools that were not making sufficient academic progress were required by the No Child Left Behind act to create a plan for improvement that had to address specific strategies to increase identified weakness areas (White, 2009). This was Ms. Riley's starting point. She challenged all of the special education teachers to individually develop their own vision and goals for the year. The teachers then convened to establish a collective vision that would support student behavior and increase understanding of new district requirements for Individual Education Program (IEP). Although these issues had divided the special education staff in the past, Ms. Riley was determined to collaborate with her team leading to success.

Step 2–Subscribe to the need to operate as a team instead of individuals.

Schools with weak cultures tend to have "silos of individuals or small isolated groups" and a "single leader who directs the work of others from a position of authority"; in contrast, strong cultures have high commitment, motivation, and cooperation among members toward achieving shared goals (Louis & Wahlstrom, 2011). In recent years, Ms. Riley noticed a "fend for yourself" environment. This, of course, led to limited success and divisions amongst the special education teachers. To combat this, Ms. Riley held non-mandatory meetings for the special education teachers. Initially, the additional meetings were met with resistance, but Ms. Riley hoped that sooner or later her staff would come to see the benefits of operating as a team.

In addition to formal team meetings, Ms. Riley even coordinated social events for her group. The extra time together resulted in the special education team getting to know each other from another perspective. Over time they began to pick up on one another's passions and personalities, strengths and weaknesses, likes and dislikes. Soon her staff began to realize that by using each other's strengths they could be more successful as a team.

Step 3–The team must develop standards.

These standards are the working norms for a team. In collaboration with her team, Ms. Riley quickly established several standards. The first was easily agreed upon—to put students first. Agreeing to this standard eliminated the tendency to allow other issues to sidetrack the team. Additional standards quickly followed: to commit to using effective IEPs, to support a full inclusion model for special education students, and to develop a vision for consistent behavior management.

Step 4–Communicate reflections.

Communication is the vehicle that drives collaboration and reflection. Ms. Riley and the team agreed to be intentional with their communication and check in with each other more frequently. The team had to learn to disagree, work through conflict and come to agreements on how to work together for the best interests of the children. The crowning achievement was the intentional positive statements the teachers expressed to their students. "Teachers who are able to implement high ratios of positive-to-negative communication behaviors with students may be especially effective teachers because they provide many teaching and learning opportunities that enhance students' meaningful engagement" (Rathel, Drasgow, Brown, & Marshall, 2013). Using this strategy yielded immediate results.

Step 5–Work collaboratively with others outside of the initial group to address barriers, challenges and problems.

Ms. Riley knew there would undoubtedly be concerns and issues needing to be addressed while transitioning students to a full inclusion model. The special education teachers and those regular education teachers who worked with special education students would need to work together, especially in addressing student behavior. Although different teachers had quite a wide range of classroom management skills, conversations and discussions with all of the teachers led to the acceptance of uniform behavioral techniques that they all agreed to implement. This consistency paid off over time and reduced the significant gap in the behavior management incidents reported by the most and least effective special education teachers.

Step 6–Assess progress to determine level of success.

Once goals were identified, the special education teachers needed to track the progress of both school and individual student goals. One portion of this process included fostering a safe learning environment (Boon et al., 2011). For example, the special education staff set a goal of lowering special education student suspensions by 40%—the previous year, their school held one of the highest special education suspension percentages in the district. Using data that was collected weekly, teachers worked together to modify their practices to create more suitable learning opportunities for students. When parents, students, and the regular education teachers observed the special education teachers working on the same page, magical things began to happen.

Step–7 Celebrate success and adjust for the rest.

Although Ms. Riley had not been accustomed to winning, the data identified several wins. When the goal of reducing suspensions was accomplished, for example, the special education department held an exclusive dance for special education students. This was a momentous event, the sense of pride and accomplishment was palpable, and the stigma of being in special education was, at least in that moment and time, finally gone. Even several regular education students asked if they could join the party, which made it especially gratifying for everyone. Ms. Riley could never have imagined these results when insisting that the special education teachers take a team approach.

The greatest win for Ms. Riley, however, was the most unexpected. When the rest of the staff began to see the success of a team approach in special education, other departments began to take steps to work within a team framework. I am sure you can imagine how the entire school culture began to shift in a positive direction. Ms. Riley should be recognized for her efforts, although we really would expect nothing less from a **SUPERHERO EDUCATOR.**

Debriefing Questions

1. List the five people you collaborate with the most.

2. List five projects you have successfully completed by collaborating with someone.

3. List five barriers to successful collaboration.

4. Do you need to be told to collaborate with your peers or does it happen naturally?

5. Reflect on the Chapter 9 Visual: Explain the picture in one sentence.

6. Observe five different educators. Record and evaluate how each teacher uses collaboration.

7. Explain two strategies for collaborating with parents.

8. Reflect on your individual gifts; how can these strengths be used to further collaboration?

9. Evaluate a business that you will not patronize because of poor collaboration. Compare and contrast that to one of your favorite businesses.

10. Explain how stellar collaboration can lead to remarkable student achievement.

Notes of Emphasis

CHAPTER 10

Dynamo Data

SUPERHERO CONNECTION

Like other citizens, Batman finds safety, comfort, and rest in his home. Unlike brick and mortar dwellings, his home is the Bat Cave. His residence is equipped with supercomputers that connect to a worldwide information network. Additionally, the Bat Cave offers surveillance capabilities, training facilities, medical resources, and a crime lab. Having this relevant information and these resources at his disposal, Batman is able to make wise, strategic decisions when battling his enemies. Teachers utilize data in much the same way. School data provides **SUPERHERO EDUCATORS** *with the power to make wise decisions.*

Impact Story

n the very popular Christmas movie *Elf*, Buddy spots a sign in New York City for the "World's Best Cup of Coffee." After tasting the coffee, an ecstatic Buddy yells, "You did it! Congratulations! World's best cup of coffee! Great job, everybody!" Next the camera pans the diner where the cup of coffee originated. Greasy food, cheap coffee, and clutter fill the screen. In a humorous manner, this scene emphasizes how organizations loudly proclaim their worth through self-promotion, with little supporting facts.

We are constantly bombarded with claims of the world's best. An ad shows the world's best chili, restaurant, videogame, car brand, mattress—even cat litter. World's Best Cat Litter is actually the name of a company that uses a patented process to compress naturally absorbent corn into concentrated granules that trap odor deep inside and form tight clumps on contact so you can do more with less litter ("World's Best Cat Litter," 2017). Fresh Step, Naturally Fresh, and Scoop Away are also companies boasting about their great cat litter products.

Consumers are left to figure out which brand actually fulfills its claims. Which brand of cat litter is the most effective? How do you know? There is a resource to help answer these kinds of questions. *Consumer Reports* is an independent, nonprofit organization that has incredible standing with the general public. Before purchasing products, conscientious buyers scour the reviews and data provided by *Consumer Reports*, which pursues its mission "by fighting to put consumers' needs first in the marketplace and by empowering them with the trusted knowledge they depend on to make better, more informed choices" ("Consumer Reports-About Us," 2017). The data provided by *Consumer Reports* is of the utmost importance for making informed purchasing decisions, allowing consumers to review all of the pertinent data and determine for themselves which product to buy.

Data propels the mission of any organization. Without data, we struggle, like Buddy the Elf, trying to decipher what the "world's best" really means. What makes the greatest school? The most effective teacher? The ultimate school leader? The highest-performing students?

Teachers make far-reaching decisions regarding their students every minute of every day. The ability to problem solve efficiently is essential, with the influences felt beyond the classroom and affecting the whole school. Beginning in 1947, W. Edwards Deming, an American working in Japan, became famous in the world of quality control. According to Deming, finding and fixing problems should be the responsibility of every employee, from the most senior manager to the person on the production line. If anyone at any level spotted a problem in the manufacturing process, Deming believed they should be encouraged and expected to stop the assembly line. W. Edwards Deming summarizes the importance of data: "In God we trust, all others must bring data" (Rhomberg, 2015).

Innovative Connections

The Apollo Education Group, the parent company of the University of Phoenix, understands the importance of data. The University of Phoenix was one of the first online universities and is currently one of the largest educational providers in the world. Over the past 20 years, it has served 2.5 million students and employs over 36,000 staff members. Data is how the University of Phoenix meets the needs of its students. Data drives student outcomes, improves retention, assists in academic success and keeps costs down. With 1,700 different courses and tens of thousands of individual pieces of content addressed to students with various learning styles coming from very different backgrounds, organization and decision-making is not only complicated but time-sensitive. Data provides a low-cost, high-return means to retain students and pull out insights about complex behaviors. Using data, the University of Phoenix is able to maintain its relevancy as a major source of adult learning (Grant, 2013).

Our schools are data rich. Our society is data rich. The challenge for organizations is to capture and use data to drive their missions. Verizon is a good example of a company that uses data and technology to create a valuable social impact. With a massive network that processes five petabytes of data per day, data is a core part of the strategy at Verizon. Data provides 360-degree views on customers, which allows advertisers to target mobile users using criteria such as ZIP codes, demographics, and interests.

Businesses must use data in creative ways in order to compete in the marketplace. Many businesses require analytics and operational capabilities to address customers, process claims and interface with devices in real time at an individual level. Delivering both analytical and operational processing to increase value, ranging from back office analytics to front office operations, is essential (Olavsrud, 2017). Computerization has made it much easier for companies to collect and analyze operational data, increase efficiency in business operations and help companies achieve maximum profitability.

One major factor in increased efficiency that has enabled companies to manage costs and operations more effectively is the ease in collecting and analyzing data regarding inventory turnover. Accurate records of total inventory, along with the ability to examine inventory turnover rates for specific items, enables a company to order supplies and manage production rates much more efficiently ("How can data assist operations management," 2015). Corporate decision makers will no longer be faced with making important business decisions based on limited data. Large amounts of information can be retrieved from data warehouses, which can be used in making strategic decisions as well as for marketing segmentation, inventory management, financial management, and sales ("Benefits of data warehouses for business," 2015).

Educational Research and Focus

When I review the portfolios of candidates for a teaching position, I ask pointed questions to reveal the true strengths and weaknesses of the candidate. I am compelled to push past the ordinary teacher responses. "I love all students." "I have high expectations for my students." "I believe every student should succeed." These are givens. All teachers want their children to succeed.

The most important question to identify a high-performing teacher is whether or not he or she can identify outstanding student progress. Data allows us to view with clarity the end results of a teacher's instruction. The complexity of teaching is well recognized; a teacher makes over 3,000 decisions daily. It is useful to think of teaching as similar to not one but several other professions, combining the skills of business management, human relations, and theater arts (Cleland, McKay, Danielson, & Axtell, 2009).

Many schools use Charlotte Danielson's Framework for Teaching—Planning and Preparation, Classroom Environment, Instructional Strategies, and Professional Responsibilities—as a guide to identify teacher quality. Having a comprehensive model such as this allows everyone to discuss teaching in the same way and communicates a strong message that the school is serious about good teaching. Great schools dialogue about teaching in this way, expecting you to use this model to examine your strengths and weaknesses. Real reflective practice defines the model. In this way, the school or district becomes a place where you develop superior teaching skills ("Teacher evaluation," 2017).

Capturing classroom and school data provides an array of information about performance. The school community values success and will continue to contribute time, energy, and resources when the data is strong. Policy makers love to develop thirty-second sound bites that highlight effective schools in their community. Parents want to brag to their co-workers, family members, and friends about their child. Without data, parents are stuck with aimless comments about how nice the teacher is or how well she dresses. Even the amount of homework and style of communication are in danger of becoming the center of conversations.

Do not force parents to struggle with finding out what is happening in the classroom and at school. Give them the data! Give them the good news! Parents will gladly spread your news because they want what is best for their child. When parents are researching schools for their children, data becomes the separator.

Student achievement is a major performance measurement. A teacher's quality is measured by how students are performing in his or her classroom. The pressure is real, which drives some teachers to limit their employment search exclusively to high socio-economic areas. The true measurement of student achievement, contrary to common belief, is not having all high marks on a report card or a full honor roll every quarter. Student growth and progress is the real benchmark. Is every student improving? Is every student progressing at a high level in your classroom?

Some students come to school with an expansive vocabulary, are ready to read, and have multiple resources to assist in learning. These students are already performing at a high level. The goal then becomes how to challenge these high-achieving students and show continual growth. On the other hand, many students will arrive in your classroom with very limited academic skills and, although they improve rapidly, still fall into the average range according to your grading standards. But your success is not measured by all of your students receiving A's. A teacher can pass out straight A's to the entire class, but that does not mean that students are progressing and achieving in the classroom.

When I was in 7th grade, my teacher would present a mini-lesson on a topic and then require the class to complete worksheets to reinforce the concepts of the lesson. Once the students completed the packet of worksheets, we were allowed free time. This meant we could chat with our friends, mix some chemicals together in the science station, or walk around the school building. I quickly mastered the task of completing mass produced textbook company worksheets. My goal was speed, and I completed the worksheets in minutes. The problem in that classroom was that student achievement was measured by worksheet completion. The finished worksheets equated to student success.

A check for understanding was missing. How were we progressing? How were we improving? I definitely knew how to complete a worksheet, but was I learning the content? Standards-based assessments are addressing these gaps in our schools, which involve measuring students' proficiency on well-defined course objectives (Marzano, 2011). Student work must be revised and reworked to gain mastery. Students build a sense of self-control as they assess, modify, and measure their own work against a set standard. Instead of entering 87% in your grade book, addressing the standard "measures characteristic properties of matter" with a descriptive assessment, "accurately measures properties of air using correct units" brings attention to what is taught and what is measured in the classroom.

SUPERHERO EDUCATORS constantly assess in the classroom to inform instruction. Formative assessments and summative assessments are administered daily. Formative assessments are evaluations given to students as teaching is taking place. If you are teaching a lesson about dividing fractions, you may pause periodically to assess what students know. This can be done orally or in written form. After you gather the data, determine whether or not it is necessary to continue teaching the concept or move on to new content because the class mastered this standard.

Summative assessments are evaluations given after teaching is completed. You teach a lesson on dividing fractions and then you hand out a worksheet or test on this standard. Both formative and summative assessments need to be used, but formative assessments should be heavily favored. Rick Stiggins ("A New Vision of Excellence in Assessment," 2017) coined the terms "for learning" and "of learning" to describe formative and summative assessments. "For learning" means we are assessing for learning's sake. These types of assessments are formative. We are acquiring data on how students are doing so we know how to adapt our teaching. In contrast, "of learning" is assessing for a grade or end point. Summative assessments are accomplished after the teaching is completed and provide data on how much of the content students have mastered. Formative and summative assessments are intended to be data checks that apprise teachers of what is happening in their classrooms.

As I was finishing up my doctoral work, I took a class centered on public policy for educational leaders. Objectives for the class revolved around public advocacy, funding principles, state law, and national education policies. Our professor was an assistant director in the United States Department of Education and had worked closely with two presidential administrations. I was confident the class would be invaluable.

The professor, disappointingly, spoke directly from his PowerPoint presentation—word for word. Each slide was jam packed with small print and lengthy, complex sentences. I attempted to ask a question to encourage him to share pertinent applications. He acknowledged my hand, but stated that all questions will have to wait until he had covered his prepared material. The class dragged on for four long hours until our highly anticipated lunch break. The professor simply read his PowerPoint slides for four hours! I have no doubt he could see a classroom filled with negative facial reactions, heads down, classmates whispering to each other, and others reading their textbooks. This was a doctoral level class full of motivated educators, and he lost us quickly. After lunch, the class continued for another four hours in the same fashion.

Of all the goals you set as an educator, student engagement is paramount. Talking is not teaching. Teaching is not standing in front of a group of students and regurgitating what you know. The complexity of teaching reaches infinitely deeper. Ensuring that all students are participating in the learning process is essential for achieving your goals. Determining what qualifies as student engagement is tricky because every student may show engagement in different ways and be actively immersed at varying times. Student involvement provides key data that serves as an indicator of achievement. Focus on your students' body language, verbal participation, attention, interactions with classmates, and enthusiasm. Look for ways to collect this data and use it to improve your instruction.

Surveys can offer useful data for improvement. Ask students about your instruction, sense of belonging, engagement level, and motivation. The results of the survey will confirm your work as a teacher or shed light on your blind spots. Results of parent surveys on homework, communication, rigor, and student achievements can be used to promote the school or as a learning tool.

Surveying people out in the community is yet another way to capture vital data. Search out data that points to school influence in the community, effects of student learning on the community, and influential school-community partnerships. Surveys provide feedback that can increase our effectiveness. The term feedback is often used to describe all kinds of comments made after the fact, including advice, praise, and evaluation, though none of these are feedback, strictly speaking. Basically, feedback is information about how we are doing in our efforts to reach a goal (Wiggins, 2012).

SUPERHERO EDUCATORS are content experts, with comprehensive knowledge in their areas of expertise. Share content related data with students, parents, and the community. Become the "go to" teacher for your subject area. Offer tips and resources to improve in your area of expertise. Produce research summaries and data to inform your audience of relevant information. Besides encouraging lifelong learning, you are dispensing vital data to improve your school community.

One of your tasks is to prepare your students for the next step of their journey. Whether it may be Kindergarten, middle school, high school or college, this preparation also includes the social skills necessary to excel at the next level. Track the progress of your students and collect the data that is pertinent to your goals. If you are a middle school teacher, tracking high school graduation rates makes sense. Gather data on how many of your students are enrolled in Advanced Placement classes. How about suspension rates? What about Honor Roll records? Literacy and math success in high school shows that you are establishing the proper foundation in middle school. Collecting and analyzing this data can be time consuming, but the benefits of utilizing this data makes the arduous task worthwhile.

Let data be your guide as you work tirelessly to increase student achievement in your classroom.

Debriefing Questions

1. Explain why data is essential for a teacher? For a school leader?

2. Evaluate this phrase: "We are a high quality school that wants all students to succeed."

3. List various forms of data that are useful to you as a teacher.

4. Reflect on Chapter 10 Visual: How has data influenced today's classrooms?

5. Provide three examples of formative assessments.

6. Give three examples of summative assessments.

7. What prevents teachers from collecting data that shows student achievement?

8. You have $1,000,000 to give away to a school. Your selection must be based on the school's data as presented on its website. Study the website of three schools and select which school would be awarded your one million dollars. Explain why you chose that school, using the data that is present on the school website.

9. Can collecting and analyzing data ever be counterproductive?

10. What types of data does your school community value?

Notes of Emphasis

CHAPTER 11
Technology Transformer

Superhero Connection

As a founding member of the Justice League, Wonder Woman has tremendous skills in hunting and combat. Her lasso of truth, indestructible bracelets, and multi-use tiara are impressive examples of technology that disrupts the status quo. What gifts and talents do you possess that lead to innovation and positive disruption?

Impact Story

In 2000, the CEO of Netflix, Reed Hastings, proposed a partnership with Blockbuster's CEO John Antioco. Netflix would run Blockbuster's online brand and Blockbuster would in turn promote Netflix in its nationwide chain of stores. John Antioco considered this start-up's offer a non-starter and felt there was no need for Blockbuster to invest in Netflix. Why would Blockbuster, with a virtual monopoly, want to partner with this pesky, new company? The rest of the story unfolded quickly. Blockbuster went bankrupt and Netflix is now a 28 billion dollar company (Satell, 2014). Netflix truly disrupted the market of home entertainment. Blockbuster, on the other hand, failed to innovate and did not react to the rapid rise of Netflix.

In my last year in college, I enrolled in a curriculum and teaching methods class. At the end of the semester we were required to purchase a small file cabinet for the neatly prepared curricula. In addition, we developed sample bulletin board themes for the various months of the school year. My young mind moved quickly forward - why not develop a file folder for every subject and every school day? A school year typically contains180 days, so I rapidly turned out curriculum plans. My goal was to fill my file cabinet with a complete set of themed units and predetermined bulletin boards. My first year of teaching, I quickly realized the foolishness of this approach. Each class is unique in its needs and brings distinct challenges to the classroom. Every student is different, requiring flexibility and possibly a whole new set of plans. I ended up scrapping the files and used the file cabinet as a stand for my boom box and cassette tapes. And a short time later, the file cabinet, boom box, and cassette tapes all were donated to a local charity. **SUPERHERO EDUCATORS** constantly innovate and technology is a tool to kick start the educational process.

Innovative Connections

Ripples is an innovative company that designed a machine to create personalized messages that transfers images onto the liquid surface of a cup of coffee. The Ripple Maker is a coffee maker sized device that connects to Wi-Fi using 3D technology, and can print designs right onto the milk foam. Customers can print a photo, personal images, or message in seconds. These messages are printed using nothing but 100% natural coffee extract ("Ripples-Make a Ripple on the World," 2017). With an app on your phone, you can creatively design your own ripple. This inventive company is using current technology to shake up the beverage industry. What if Starbucks charged five cents more for each coffee that enlisted a personalized message?

Examples of disruptive innovations abound. Take, for example, Salesforce. com, which has rattled the technology world through new cloud storage organizations and systems. Salesforce is revolutionizing the way businesses manage customer relationships. Cloud computing is quickly replacing the traditional model of having software applications installed on site. So as opposed to working in isolation, an entire company can work as one team. With cloud computing, businesses access applications via the internet ("What is Cloud Computing?" 2017).

Then again, there's Uber. Only a few years ago, taxis and mass transportation were the primary transportation options for people without their own cars. Uber quickly disrupted the transportation market. Uber Technologies provides a smartphone application that connects drivers with people who need a ride. The company's application enables users to arrange and schedule transportation and/or logistics services with third party providers (Bloomberg-Company Overview of Uber," 2017).

Cambridge Analytica earned serious bragging rights as the data firm that helped engineer Donald Trump's victory in the United States presidential election. Cambridge's pitch is that it divides audiences into "psychographic groups" to target them with the kinds of messages that, like most ads, are based on demographic factors but also are most likely to appeal to their emotional and psychological profiles. Cambridge will continue to harvest data on the American electorate (Lapowsky, 2017).

How do you receive the latest news or up to date information? Twitter may be the most popular water cooler ever, a place to discuss current events and topics. Though its user base is dwarfed by Facebook, no social network has quite the influence of Twitter. So, what better way to assess its impact than with one of its strongest conventions - the hashtag? Before Twitter, the # key was little more than something found on telephones to denote "number or pound". Now hashtags are the definitive way to group tweets on the same subject. Businesses stay connected to Twitter, posting positive news and watching in fear of a complaint going viral. A wave of negative tweets can deeply embarrass a business. It can be a remarkably effective way of making a company change its policy. Meanwhile, on the financial markets, many have started using social media to predict the future value of businesses. By analyzing the "firehose" (that is, all the tweets from everyone), researchers say they can make an educated guess over how stocks may perform (Lee, 2013).

Numerous other examples could easily be found, but the pattern is clear. Technological innovations often have the power to disrupt the status quo. Unfortunately, technology seems to have had a relatively minor impact on the way we teach and the way students learn, in large part because of the many barriers education faces in using innovative technology to increase student achievement. These obstacles range from funding, priorities, expertise, time, workload, to downright fear. A personal revolution of technology must occur in each classroom. How can you positively disrupt the learning of students by using technology? **SUPERHERO EDUCATORS** blast away the barriers and use groundbreaking technology to rescue students from the villains of low engagement and disinterest.

Educational Research and Focus

If you were told you were disrupting class when you were in school, you were probably demonstrating a negative behavior, maybe talking to your neighbor about your favorite sports team while the teacher was explaining a concept. Disrupting the status quo in this way is obviously not a good thing. However, disrupting the status quo in different ways is desperately needed in our schools. Ask yourself, why we are doing what we are doing? With online grading, teacher websites, and social media, do we really need face to face parent/teacher conferences? Isn't there a better way to foster parent and school relationships? Why do we hold professional development days in the middle of the week and send students home early to households that may well not have a parent present? Are half days necessary? Why are teacher observations done only once or twice a year? Do the hours that students are in school make sense for optimal learning? Can technology relieve the burden of homework? Other questions naturally follow as we push against the status quo in our schools.

The theory of disruptive innovation was first put forth by Harvard professor Clayton M. Christensen in his research on the disk-drive industry. The theory explains the phenomenon by which an innovation transforms an existing market through the introduction of simplicity, convenience, accessibility, and affordability, resulting in a better produce that is more widely available to larger markets than the technology the innovation replaced. This is a positive force for both education and society ("Christensen Institute-Disruption Innovation," 2017).

In education, as discussed in Chapter 9, collaboration and building strong networks of fellow teachers is essential. Korzeniowski (2016) details the importance that Tony Hsieh, CEO of Zappos, places on collaboration. CEO Hsieh places a premium on prioritized collisions over convenience, meaning he wants workers to run into each other during their normal work routine. The rationale is that a casual conversation can quickly turn into a formal exchange in which outstanding problems find solutions. The culture of Zappos focuses on how to provide a vision to motivate, remove obstacles so others can achieve goals, and foster a community that works well together. Modern teams in technology do not work well in top-down hierarchies. Collaboration often achieves better results.

Just as collaboration is essential, so too is, competition. Unfortunately, competition has gotten a bad reputation in our schools. Recently, I visited a classroom where a poster was prominently positioned in the front of the room stating, "Collaboration is the key to success, not competition." This poster captured my attention because I disagree.

I believe we need both collaboration and competition in our schools. When I was in middle school, we were assigned several group projects. Our teacher would review the rubric and remind the class that all students in a group would receive the same grade. Quickly, I smiled and thought through this concept. I am in a group of five and three of the members of my group never receive a grade lower than an A minus. Therefore, my only contribution will be cracking jokes about our classmates. Even as my jokes were not well received, I was confident in my final grade for this assignment.

As the members of my team complained to the teacher about my lack of motivation and desire to just make fun of people the entire time, my teacher said it was the group's responsibility to force me to participate fully. What were the members of the group going to do? Without the ability to penalize or levy consequences, collaboration without competition is not effective. My final grade was an A, with signing my name as my lone contribution to the project.

Find a way to inject competition alongside collaboration and you have the recipe for success. Instead of awarding the same grade to each member of the group, instill a personal commitment into the assignment. Every student will be responsible for a section or every student must record his or her role on the project. Require team members to write a narrative on the contributions of each other, including themselves. Develop an individual assessment that tests the knowledge of each group member. Thinking through all objectives of the assignment and group dynamics forges a partnership between collaboration and competition. Encourage students to compete against themselves and others in a healthy manner. Competition is not a dirty word, but a strong motivator. Students should compete to be first in the spelling bee, the one chosen for the newspaper article, and down the road the one to be awarded the scholarship money. Disrupt school practices by integrating both competition and collaboration in meaningful ways.

For over fifty years, we have implemented parent/teacher conferences in the same fashion. Parents come to the school building and meet with the classroom teacher for ten to fifteen minutes. By the time introductions are completed and the teacher reviews the student's grades, the session is completed. With the ease of access to online grading, teacher websites, and other communication tools, this way of collaborating with parents is outdated. Without a strong focus and strategy, these conferences struggle to produce positive outcomes. Progressive schools permit adaptations that show promise, such as student led conferences and allotting longer blocks of time to spend with parents.

The best disrupters to traditional parent-teacher conferences are called Academic Parent Teacher Teams (APTT). With APTTs, parents meet as a group with a classroom teacher for 75 to 90 minutes three times during the school year. At each meeting, parents discuss the expectations or standards for their child's grade, see data about their child's performance, set a 60-day academic goal for their child, and then practice strategies to implement at home. Between the first and second group meeting, parents meet one-on-one with their child's teacher for 30 minutes to discuss their progress. Technology tips and new learning tools can be taught to parents and transferred into the home. The early results of this new shift in conferences is positive: increased attendance, renewed parent empowerment, improved use of time, and increased father involvement (Paredes, 2010).

Schools around our country are woefully behind in disruptive innovation. If you started a school today, how would you design the building? How would the classrooms be configured? What innovations would the curriculum include? How would you capitalize on the technologies available at your fingertips?

Some schools are beginning to discover the benefits of electronic tablets and even smartphones. As more technology tools make sense for learning, teachers need to make decisions toward implementation. Dr. Ruben Puentedura developed the SAMR (Substitution, Augmentation, Modification, Redefinition) model as a way for teachers to evaluate how they are incorporating technology into their instructional practice. *Substitution* simply involves using technology that directly replaces traditional tools when, for example, students write essays or assignments on a computer rather than using the traditional pencil and paper. *Augmentation* takes place when technology is used as a substitute in a way that involves functional improvement, as when students use a computer's spell-checking function. *Modification* involves using technology to significantly change the classroom, as when students collaborate on an assignment using Google Docs. Finally, *redefinition* takes place when technology completely replaces traditional methods and assignments and assessments are conducted entirely through digital means ("Ruben Puentedura," 2017).

By incorporating this model into your lesson plans, teachers can begin to foster higher levels of student learning and produce greater motivation to learn.

Researching and analyzing technology applications for the classroom can be overwhelming as you filter through the many options. Decisions have to be made on cost, usage, and overall value. Start with the end in mind. Think about how the specific technology will further the teaching standard. If the teaching standard demands student proficiency in multiplication, what technology tools can assist in this goal? The lesson objectives drive the need for integrating technology. Without this focus on the standards and objectives first, teachers may find themselves using creative and engaging technology in the classroom with little connection to the curriculum.

One example of a fun activity that I witnessed in a classroom involved cookies and crackers. The students were very excited to work with the food products. After thirty minutes of observing the lesson, I struggled to see the link to the state standards or classroom objectives. I asked the teacher what I was missing, she responded that her students have always loved this lesson and remember it year after year. There was no mention of how the cookies and crackers assist in the transfer of new knowledge.

Teachers need to develop engaging and memorable lessons, but the lessons must originate from the standards and objectives, not the other way around. If the standard states that students must be able to multiply two digit numbers, the goal is to create an engaging lesson that teaches students how to master this standard effectively. Use the intense attachment students today have with their cell phones and tablets by taking advantage of the many online learning opportunities. The Khan Academy offers free online lessons and practice opportunities in the form of videos. Other websites and online platforms present information that parents and children can use to enhance classroom learning.

Personalized learning is a great disrupter of the status quo that has potential to meet the needs of all learners. Focus on an individual growth plan for every student. Challenge every student and adapt the curriculum to his or her needs. View novel technology as a partner, and personalized learning as a path to student growth.

SUPERHERO EDUCATORS transform with technology and look for meaningful ways to disrupt the traditional classroom. Think about how your personal talents can assist with improving lessons to match the needs of today's learners. Be bold in your new efforts and look for continual improvements. Continuing to use the same methods and procedures, is not an option. Initiate positive change with purpose and be a technology transformer.

Debriefing Questions

1. How has education changed in the last 5 years?

2. What impact has technology had on education?

3. How is teaching and learning different today than when you were in 6th grade?

4. What needs to be disrupted in education to meet the needs of more students?

5. Can there be too much change in education? Explain.

6. Does technology level the playing field for all students? Explain.

7. What are the most innovative uses of technology in classrooms? Are they effective?

8. What role does competition have in the educational system?

9. Reflect on Chapter 11 Visual: What is one outdated educational practice that must be changed?

10. How does a teacher thrive in a school environment where change is constant?

Notes of Emphasis

CHAPTER 12

Perceptive Performer

Superhero Connection

Black Panther is a superhero that specializes in unarmed combat. He is a skilled tracker, inventor, strategist, and performer of African martial arts. His overwhelming effectiveness stems from his deft use of acrobatics and stunning physical maneuvers. **SUPERHERO EDUCATORS** *not only master their content, but also are true performers in the classroom.*

Impact Story

Recently, I listened to the comedian Kevin Hart as he entertained thousands of people. The crowd was so large it entirely filled a small stadium. Kevin's timing, facial expressions, vocal inflections, and volume were perfect. Even if you do not value his material and messaging, one cannot deny the sheer brilliance of his performance. Highly effective teachers are also performers, just in the classroom setting instead of on a stage. They know their audience and perform effectively to maximize student results.

Rodney Dangerfield was a famous comedian and actor starting in the 1940's until his death in 2004. Some of his favorite lines are still funny today:

"My wife and I were happy for twenty years. Then we met."

"I could tell that my parents hated me. My bath toys were a toaster and a radio."

"My mother had morning sickness after I was born."

Rodney's creativity, timing, expressions, and ability to know his audience made him a true comedic legend. Today, this brilliant talent is evident in another humorist, Chris Rock: "I used to work at McDonald's making minimum wage. You know what that means when someone pays you minimum wage? You know what your boss was trying to say? 'Hey if I could pay you less, I would, but it's against the law.'"

"You don't pay taxes. They take taxes."

"Charlie Brown is the one person I identify with. C.B. is such a loser. He wasn't even the star of his own Halloween special." ("GoodReads Quotes," 2017).

By studying famous comedians, teachers can learn ways to connect with students through active performance. Learn how these performers use their voice and body to keep their audience spellbound, wanting more.

Innovative Connections

The performance of smart technology for the home is nothing short of amazing. Home thermostats, cameras, and smoke detectors link directly to smartphones. From the office to the commute home, you can adjust the temperature at home, view what is happening in your kitchen, and access live reports regarding your smoke and CO_2 detectors. Smart technology brings convenience, efficiency, and savings to more and more people. Nearly all facets of our life will soon be connected through smart technology. From turning on lights, to daily commutes, to our work environments, our world will be routed through our smartphones. Performance matters! Just as we have come to expect and demand performance from our household items, we have come to treasure this efficacy in the rest of our lives.

This same priority for performance exists in education. Children depend upon teachers who can plan, integrate technology, and work collaboratively. Just as important as those qualities, however, is the actual performance of the teacher in action. **SUPERHERO EDUCATORS** incorporate into their performance their ability to understand, motivate, manage, inspire, and achieve excellence with their students.

Educational Research and Focus

SUPERHERO EDUCATORS are true performers in the classroom. They continually come up with creative solutions to classroom challenges. The delivery of content is timed well for absorption and retention. Facial expressions and body movements are performed intentionally to maximize learning. Each student in the classroom is known on a personal level, generating a lasting and relevant connection to content.

My high school years were great, and life-long friends and wonderful memories were made during those four short years. But I had little thought for the future. Immediately after the graduation ceremony, we stood in line to receive smiles, hugs, and words of congratulations. One of my favorite teachers came through the line, gave me a hug, and told me that I should become a teacher. Before the day was over, two more teachers echoed the same sentiment. I met that strange plea each time with a smile and a laugh. Didn't my teachers remember me as a student? Just a few days ago, I was in their class, challenging course content, spouting "humorous" jokes out loud, and constantly flirting with the girls. Why were they recruiting me for the teaching profession? Being an adult in no way related to my immature high school persona. With nothing much else to do, however, by the end of the summer I had decided to follow a friend to a teacher's college to give it a shot.

During those pivotal college years, I frequently questioned my future profession because of the traditional structure of the classes and total lack of innovation and creativity in the college curriculum. I could write a compelling ten-page paper on the psychology of learning or classroom management, but did that mean that I would in actuality be an effective educator?

Being a master of content is absolutely essential for high-performing educators, but just as essential is what you do with that content. Possessing an astute understanding of literature, music, and history is nowhere near the same as teaching these subjects to twenty to thirty young people with varying abilities and experiences.

SUPERHERO EDUCATORS are top-notch performers. They know how to read their students' facial expression, and body language and respond accordingly. Daily, they set the mood and proactively orchestrate an outstanding educational performance. Determining when to be assertive, when to incorporate humor, and when to choose a battle, all the while teaching the content well is a minute by minute challenge.

Proper questioning is one kind of performance. Pulling answers out of students is truly an art form. Ask questions designed to help students obtain a deeper understanding of content, which will increase interest in the topic ("Four Types of Questions that Increase Rigor", 2015). Be mindful of the level of difficulty and the number of questions you are asking. Strike a balance between questions that are basic, fact driven in nature, and those that require a higher level of academic sophistication and abstract thought. Expertise in asking questions leads to strong student motivation to learn and develops keener awareness of the content.

Bloom's Taxonomy assists educators in planning and developing lessons by identifying teaching goals. These six teaching goals are listed from the simple to the complex: Remember, Understand, Apply, Analyze, Evaluate, and Create. If all teacher questions and assignments are at the simple stage of *Remember*, students will never move to higher level thinking and abstract concepts. By sharing a variety of goals along Bloom's Taxonomy, students will benefit from the intentional planning and be more engaged in learning (Armstrong, 2017). Teaching is complex. Effective teachers emphasize meaning. They encourage students to respond to questions and activities that require them to discover and assimilate their own understanding, rather than to simply memorize material (Stronge, 2012).

Enable students to visualize while you teach by choosing words that create mental images. **SUPERHERO EDUCATORS** deliver content in a manner that paints a vivid picture for learners. Humans are intensely visual beings. Our eyes send millions of signals every second along the optic nerves to the visual processing centers of the brain. It is not surprising that the visual components of a memory are so robust. Although each of us has the ability to process kinesthetic and auditory information, we take in more information visually than through any other sense. The capacity for long-term memory of pictures seems almost unlimited (Wolfe, 2010). Do you remember reading children's stories, your favorite fables, or Bible parables? A story is a powerful way of illustrating a particular point because it triggers the mind's eye and jumpstarts long term memory. Let students visualize what you are teaching and use this powerful tool to help them acquire long-term knowledge.

In fifth grade, I wondered why Howie, an eighth grader, was not passing the basketball more often during our recess pick-up games. I expressed my frustration with Howie. He grabbed me by the shirt and slowly recited, "Pick your battles, Chump." Immediately, I realized that I truly did not mind running up and down the basketball court the entire recess without a ball ever being passed to me. It was all about picking my battles, and this was not the time to engage in combat.

Minus the threat, Howie's advice is sound for today's classrooms. Pick your battles as a teacher. This does not mean that your classroom is void of organization and discipline. Also, this does not provide an excuse to let students control your classroom. Picking your battles means consistently discerning when student behavior absolutely crosses the line and when student actions are not that big of a deal. As the teacher, you hold the power in the classroom. You are blessed with outstanding gifts that can positively impact children's lives. There will be numerous daily challenges, but you can find real solutions. Consistently select the battles that are essential and imperative to students' growth.

Teacher leaders are selective in their battles, knowing when to take a stand and when to retreat. Classroom management is especially difficult because it cannot be reduced to a formula. Children and the environment around them are dynamic. Often times student behavior has nothing to do with you as a teacher. Constant disruptions or inattentiveness may have nothing to do with your lessons or management strategies.

The issue of equity comes into play in these situations. Traditionally, teachers set up their classroom environments centered on equality. Every student is treated exactly the same way. This of course makes sense, but we also need to focus on what is fair to each students, namely equity. Through personalized instruction, each student essentially has his or her own individual learning plan. As we perform in our classroom both equity and equality are essential, but mainly we should strive for equity. Personalizing the classroom lets every student maximize his or her potential. Some people see equity as lowering the expectations for students. The opposite is true as students understand equity allows them to be treated as a unique individuals, which serves as a motivator.

Alex missed his first assignment of the school year because he was at the hospital all night with his grandma. As a teacher, you could punish him for not being prepared or you could understand the uniqueness of the situation and develop a plan of action. Equity dictates that you individually work with Alex to ensure he completes the goals of that missed assignment but is not punished for being with his grandma at the hospital.

You have a reputation as an educator. Parents, students, colleagues, and others talk about you and your performance as a teacher. What do you want your reputation to be? Spend time and energy on perfecting your instructional techniques and mastering the curriculum. Practice again and again to perform at a high level. Referring back to the comedian analogy, the time spent practicing is enormously important. In total amazement, I watch Kevin Hart's comedy routine. His facial techniques and delivery are so good, it seems like he is talking directly to me. That is exactly what is required for great teaching.

When you witness a highly effective educator in action, you know that person is exceptional. Be exceptional and share with others the talking points of your skills. If you are really good at taking a complex concept and putting it into simpler terms, videotape the session. Make your school parents and other stakeholders aware of your educator strengths. Be a positive person who strives for harmony, then promote the effects and benefits of this talent. Tremendous performers promote the positive. Without denying reality, they always see the glass as half full.

Reframing is a technique for looking at reality that allows you to see things in a new light, to sort out facts and ideas so the positive ones emerge into clarity, while the negatives, though not forgotten, are placed on the back burner (Kline & Saunders, 2010). Become the teacher that students talk about twenty years from now. Be the educator who students proclaim transformed their lives. Do not be a generalist that tries to do all things. Continue to hone your skills as an educator.

SUPERHERO EDUCATORS are able to perform with all students. Embrace the challenges and opportunities of diversity by operating through a new lens.

Expect the best from all students and uphold strong expectations. Teacher expectations regarding the potential of academic success for individual students are a critical factor in student achievement. Expect students of color, as well as those from lower socioeconomic groups, to perform well in your class. All students work hard and grow in the expert performer's classroom!

Students under your instruction need to be able to read, think critically, compute, and problem solve. Sitting behind a podium and reading PowerPoint slides to students is not teaching. Almost anyone can perform the role of teacher in that situation. You could be replaced easily if that was the case. Reading from a textbook and telling stories to your students is not teaching. That is an example of storytelling that almost anyone can do - you can be replaced in this scenario, too! Starting the class with an engaging and applicable story, proposing thoughtful questions, leading students to research primary sources, developing critical thought through individualized instructional goals, and fostering varied assessment skills is true teaching. Proper pacing, higher level questioning, humor, individualized attention, picking battles, and energy is all part of the performance. Teach in ways that emphasize your strengths and natural talents. People will quickly notice and appreciate your value by telling others about the high quality performance they witnessed. Taking a risk by performing may be scary or intimidating. Always take a chance on better, even if it seems threatening (Catmull, 2014). Master your performance as a **SUPERHERO EDUCATOR.**

Debriefing Questions

1. Why is it important for teachers to be connected with their students?

2. In what ways can you connect to your students to improve your performance in the classroom?

3. Observe the two most effective teachers in your school. How do these teachers connect with students?

4. What are the barriers to being connected with students?

5. What tools and strategies prepare you to be a high performer in the classroom?

6. Think about your professional strengths. How do these strengths assist you in becoming a superior performer in the classroom?

7. List examples of previous teachers who were top notch educational performers and explain what qualities they possessed.

8. Engagement is a tremendous outcome of high performance educators. How do you measure student engagement?

9. How do you improve your performance as a teacher?

10. Can you be a highly effective teacher and not be good as a performer in the classroom? Explain.

Notes of Emphasis

CHAPTER 13
Superhuman Health

Superhero Connection

"It's a bird! It's a plane! It's Superman!" These were my favorite phrases as a child. I thought Superman could do anything. There are many superheroes, but Superman was far and away my favorite. Shockingly, I had never heard of kryptonite until watching the Superman movie. Kryptonite is Superman's only weakness, causing him to lose his super powers. **SUPERHERO EDUCATORS** *perform spectacular feats inside the classroom every day. They have only one kryptonite. Their personal health is the primary element that can prevent a* **SUPERHERO EDUCATOR** *from accomplishing great victories.*

Impact Story

Your health matters! **SUPERHERO EDUCATORS**, unfortunately, will too often put the needs of others before themselves. They tend to skip breakfast or lunch, eat unhealthy foods, drink too much alcohol, fail to exercise, go to bed too late at night, ignore health problems, and are too busy to go to the doctor. I am as guilty as anyone else. I am not proud of doing many of these unhealthy actions during my career. I too often put myself last—just like many of the other **SUPERHERO EDUCATORS**.

Superman had one weakness—kryptonite. **SUPERHERO EDUCATORS** have their own kryptonite—personal wellness. We typically disregard the normal things we need to do to stay healthy. Then, BOOM!—something happens that forces us to pay attention to our health. Although health problems come in many different forms, if not managed properly, they can prevent us from being great. A health problem is not necessarily a death sentence, but we need to have a plan to effectively manage our own professional kryptonite.

At the time of writing this chapter, I was diagnosed with diabetes. The diagnosis sent me into a brief stint of depression. I can only be upset with myself. For years I did not eat breakfast because I was rushing out of the house. I rarely ate lunch because I was too busy. I snacked on unhealthy food from the end of the school day to bedtime, only to repeat the same poor choices again the following day.

These unhealthy practices add up over time, and our bodies suffer the consequences. I know you want to be great for a long time. I am begging all **SUPERHERO EDUCATORS** to please take care of their health. Put deliberate procedures in place that will lead to a healthy lifestyle. You can do it. Be a healthy superhero inside and outside the classroom!

Innovative Connections

Employee wellness has received increasing emphasis from businesses over the years, and the wellness environment today is totally different than it was when I was a new classroom teacher. I had good health insurance but did not have the tools to maintain a healthy lifestyle.

Although employee and workplace wellness programs have been around for decades, such initiatives in governmental organizations typically lag behind initiatives in the private sector in both magnitude and diversity. The range of programs and services is far more sophisticated in the corporate world than in public agencies (Otenyo & Smith, 2017). Nonetheless, an emphasis on wellness is becoming more and more common, even in public institutions.

One increasingly popular component of wellness programs is the use of monetary incentives to reward workers for participating in wellness activities or achieving particular health outcomes. Half of the major employers in the U.S. offered wellness programs and incentives for participating (Claxton et al., 2015). Wellness incentives have become more and more common as programs have expanded their measurement of outcomes through health risk assessments and biometric screening. This is smart for employers. Healthy workers should equate to greater productivity.

As employers in both the public and private sectors have gained experience with wellness programs, several do's and don'ts have emerged. The do's include: do engage the appropriate stakeholders, do support employees to be their best self, do remember that changing human behavior is not easy, and do celebrate success, even if it feels small. The don'ts include: don't assume you know what employees want, don't consider your online portal and fitness discount a wellness program, don't host the biggest loser, and don't be the wellness police (Ceccherini, 2016). This is the blueprint many organizations use. Over time, following these guidelines can lead to a healthier workforce.

Kohl's, a retail department store, recently built a wellness center near their headquarters in Wisconsin. The new wellness center has a full-size pharmacy run by CVS Caremark and a full-service medical clinic with twelve treatment rooms operated by Columbia St. Mary's Hospital. The fitness center, operated by the Wisconsin Athletic Club, takes up the entire second floor at 14,000 square feet. Kohl's employees can join for $25 per month or pay an additional fee to use any Wisconsin Athletic Club facility. But either way, Kohl's will pick up the tab if employees use the facilities at least eight times per month (Davis, 2014).

Many companies have a similar policy of matching the fee of a gym membership if the employee visits the facility on a regular basis. Our local public school district has an employee wellness department, which offers a wide range of supports and services for their employees in three general categories.

First, the department offers strategies aimed to assist employees personally—support for cancer survivors, diabetes prevention, mental health counseling, tobacco prevention, legal aid consultation, and deductibles to cover prescribed medication.

Second, opportunities are offered onsite at local schools. This comes in the form of wellness seminars, after-school group exercise programs, and healthy cooking classes taught as part of professional development.

Third is the opportunity to pay reduced rates for local gym memberships. Employees can earn a $20 monthly reimbursement towards a gym membership fee if the employee attends twelve times per month. All of these efforts support the employees to be their best self on and off the job. It is wise for **SUPERHERO EDUCATORS** to take advantages of these opportunities.

Educational Research and Focus

Hopefully, after reading this chapter so far, you have thought about the status of your own health, which can and will impact your ability to be great. A healthy diet is the recipe for a well-functioning body. Food is the source of energy for all of our bodily functions and directly affects how our bodies and minds function at every stage of life. A healthy diet is important for a variety of reasons, including disease prevention, maintenance of a healthy weight and quality of life (Hanes, 2017).

Educators having successful diets becomes very challenging. I am not a nutritionist, and have made many nutritional mistakes. The mistake I am most guilty of is not eating breakfast before going to work. This problem occurs for several reasons, the primary one being poor time management, which led to rushing many mornings. Simply, there was not enough time to eat.

Everyone reading this book knows what the simple solution to this should be. Let's say it all together: "Wake up earlier!" **SUPERHERO EDUCATORS**, set your alarm clocks fifteen minutes earlier. This will give you the extra minutes you will need to make breakfast. We have been told by too many experts that breakfast is the most important meal of the day. I understand that now and make it a point to eat something before I walk out of the door every morning.

If poor time management is preventing you from eating breakfast in the morning, complete some tasks the night before, including ironing your clothes, making the children's lunches, and organizing your work bag. I usually pick out my clothes for the week on Sunday, which gives me a few extra minutes to spare each morning. Also, I try to go to bed earlier so it does not feel like I am changing my sleeping habits to steal time in the morning.

I have heard too many educators say they were too busy during the school day to eat. Once again, I used to be super guilty of this diet crime. Many days I brought a bag lunch but still did not eat because I was too busy. Please give yourself permission to eat lunch. The work is not going away if you eat lunch or don't each lunch.

I am not the biggest fan of eating school prepared lunch. That is nothing against the great people who prepare school lunches; it just was not a practice I participated in often. Others swear by school lunches and take advantage of the convenience for their schedule. They have developed a routine, which works well for them. It really does not matter which lunch option you prefer. Just make sure that you give yourself permission to eat lunch.

Some educators like to eat snacks all day long. An elementary principal ate chips every time she joined an Individualized Education Plan (IEP) meeting. The school had a special education population that was forty percent of the total school population. Basically, this meant she was in an IEP meeting most school days, which also meant she was eating chips all of the time. If you feel the need to snack all day, make your options healthier choices. Some suggestions for snacking include fruits, veggies, and granola.

Remember, you can't be a **SUPERHERO EDUCATOR** on an empty stomach.

Getting the appropriate amount of sleep is essential. A Gallup poll in 2013 found that 40% of Americans get less than the recommended seven to nine hours of sleep nightly. By contrast, in 1942, 84% of adults slept at least 7 to 9 hours at night (Gaines, 2016). A more common reason for not getting a good night's sleep is obviously staying up too late or taking too much work home. Make a commitment to yourself and to the education profession. Get your work done at a reasonable time, turn off your phone, turn off your TV and allow yourself to get enough sleep.

Please review your sleeping patterns. Identify the time you think is the most appropriate time for you to go to sleep. Also, identify the time you think is most appropriate time for you to wake up in the morning. Make a commitment to stick to this schedule. Try it for several weeks. This will do wonders and help you maintain **SUPERHERO EDUCATOR** status.

Many educators report that they are losing sleep because of anxiety and stress. I know this is an issue but didn't realize how big of an issue this was until recently. I happened to be in a casual conversation with eight principals, and the concept of anxiety and stress came up in our discussion. Six of the eight principals were on medicine to control their anxiety and stress. If this is as typical as I suspect it is, we have a serious health problem in our profession.

Stress is a silent killer. Unfortunately, too many people are not even aware of the fact that they are living with significant stress. Ferrier (2016) suggests using the Pedasky model to help identify thoughts that trigger stress. Define the situation. Write down your thoughts. Identify your emotions. Write down your physical sensations. Document any resulting behaviors. I hope this helps you with your quest as it helps me understand and manage my own level of stress.

Stress can have a significant negative effect on you as a teacher. The first sign of this is often ineffective classroom management. Your patience will be significantly reduced, and you will become increasingly frustrated with the students you serve. This creates a negative environment for students, which can easily lead to classroom management issues. Geving (2007) found inappropriate student behavior is the leading cause of stress for teachers. Being an educator is very difficult, and not managing stress can make your job impossible to manage, damage your relationships with your colleagues and even affect your chances of promotion—not fair but true.

I have always wondered why educators avoid going to the doctor. Cost may be a factor for some. When I was a brand new teacher, medical insurance covered all medical expenses. Today, visiting a doctor may involve a significant out of pocket expense. Some educators do not go to the doctor because they fear getting bad news. Finally, being too busy is the leading reason I hear educators say why they do not regularly see the doctor. In the past I had been super guilty of this. I have often heard people say it is a busy time in the school year. The weakest excuse I have heard is, "I will go to the doctor during the summer time." What happens if the summer time is too late?

The bottom line is we must take care of our health and this means going to the doctor, eating breakfast, reducing stress, and managing of time. Your classroom existed before you and will exist after you are long gone. Part of your professional responsibility is taking care of your health. If you want to be a **SUPERHERO EDUCATOR**, drop the excuses. Take care of yourself and be the healthiest teacher you can possibly be.

Debriefing Questions

1. Give an example of when you needed to go to the doctor but did not.

2. Describe your eating habits. Do you have a healthy or unhealthy diet?

3. List three barriers that stop you from having good sleeping habits.

4. Ask three of your colleagues how often they go to the doctor. Did their responses surprise you?

5. Does your school have a wellness program? Describe its key components.

6. What features of your wellness program have you taken advantage of at your school?

7. Observe five educators. Record and evaluate how they handle stress.

8. Are you the type who recognizes when you are stressed out or does someone else recognize it before you do? Evaluate.

9. How do you manage your stress levels and stay productive on your job?

10. Reflect on Chapter 13 Visual: Describe when you have experienced reduced effectiveness because of health reasons.

Notes of Emphasis

CHAPTER 14

Skyrocketing Success

Superhero Connection

Batman is one of our most famous superheroes. He also has a partner that supports him when the going gets tough. Robin is a key contributor to the success of Batman. I look at Robin as an extra set of eyes for Batman. Batman and Robin collaborate on best strategies, which often leads to success. When the enemy is defeated, Robin always has a key role. Batman would not have been as successful without the help of his partner Robin.

Impact Story

When you have a child, the transition between diapers and wearing big kid underwear is an amazing process. I am not sure who feels more excited, the parents or the child. This can also be an incredibly frustrating time for all stakeholders. Reflecting upon my own children's experiences, I recall the following challenges: refusal to use the adult sized toilet, numerous occasions of not quite being able to make it to the toilet in time, accidents in the shopping mall, and failure to ask if they needed to use the bathroom before loading them into the car.

There are several theories on how to effectively potty train. Many believe that one gender is easier to train than the other. I am not sure if I believe that. In my experience, it was a struggle with both genders. Every time we made one step forward, it seemed that we took four steps back. Two situations personally drove me crazy. First, my children would use the toilet consistently and without problem at their day care. Then they would come home and have accidents. This was extremely humbling and left me wondering what I was doing wrong. Second, my kids would spend the weekend at their grandparent's house and have no issues using the bathroom. When they came home, however, we reverted back to frequent accidents.

To keep my sanity, I needed a new strategy. This is where the art of celebration came in handy. We had not been celebrating bathroom successes—which both the day care and their grandparents were doing. I am a quick learner, so I developed a chart that would be used to document successful toileting. At home, a successful trip to the potty turned into a celebration.

I was surprised how much toddlers enjoy the structure and praise of charting success. Rewards included the happy dance, songs, high fives, and favorite snacks. Frustrations eased once we started celebrating successes.

Pick an area where you experience frustrations and start celebrating success. Watch the transformation that will take place.

Innovative Connections

During my first year of teaching, I also worked at Best Buy, a multi-channel consumer electronics retailer with stores in the US, Canada, and Mexico. Founded by Richard Schulze and Gary Smoliak in 1966, Best Buy has more than 1,900 stores and locations today, including large-format and Best Buy Mobile stores. The company also offers technical support under the Geek Squad brand (Bailey, 2015).

I started working at Best Buy for the employee discount and to earn a little extra money. Witnessing the way they celebrated successes truly impacted my teaching. Best Buy celebrates success in two areas: department sales and Performance Service Plans (PSP) sales. The managers clearly emphasized that the overall goal was to sell more on this day than the same day in the previous year by tracking historical data. While we were working, management tried to motivate us to make each day a successful one. Exceeding sales from the prior year was celebrated during staff meetings by public recognition and small prizes. I really enjoyed being part of the team when my sales contributed to a winning day.

A PSP is an extended warranty contract to repair or replace an item due to operational failure. It is generally sold as an add-on product and covers a specific duration of time in return for the premium paid. Extended warranties sometimes offer additional service options or more flexible terms than the manufacturer's original warranty (Lewis, 2017). I was embarrassed when I didn't have any PSPs on a particular night but my co-workers did. Acknowledgements of PSPs sold were announced daily and monthly. During staff meetings, monthly leaders were showcased and highlighted by the store manager.

While all this excitement was occurring when I was working in the evenings at Best Buy, I began to notice during the day that we were not celebrating the successes of students at my school in the same way. I thought it was weird that a business organization was celebrating successes, but not a learning organization. Obviously the business world knew something that we in the educational world did not know—or, worse yet, knew and were not practicing.

Educational Research and Focus

Ms. Carlton was a veteran teacher with over twenty years of teaching experience. She had a sound grasp of the curriculum and knew effective teaching strategies. On a percentage basis, Ms. Carlton had more students with perfect attendance than any other homeroom teacher, but there was no school wide policy to celebrate reaching this milestone. Although other teachers celebrated this achievement in their own ways, Ms. Carlton did not think it was necessary to celebrate her students that had perfect attendance. She felt that having perfect attendance was the expectation and that there was, therefore, no need for celebration. But her students with perfect attendance heard about the other classes' recognitions and began to feel that Ms. Carlton did not care. Several parents complained to the principal about Ms. Carlton's seeming lack of interest in the success of her students. Based on these complaints, parents began to ask that their kids not be assigned to Ms. Carlton's room.

Ms. Carlton's struggled with poor classroom skills. Because of her inability to maintain a productive classroom environment, the more difficult students were intentionally placed in the other 4th grade classrooms with better management, although she never knew her class was hand-picked for her. As usual, the school year started off well, and the behavior of her students was just fine.

By November, however, her classroom was out of control and dangerous. Because Ms. Carlton refused to reinforce her students for proper behavior, the only way students could get her attention was to act up in class. Even those students who typically had not displayed behavior problems in the past began to misbehave. Her colleagues encouraged Ms. Carlton to change her classroom culture by highlighting students that were making positive behavior choices. Ms. Carlton refused. Her students continued to have no positive incentive to behave appropriately and stopped caring, especially when they saw other students being positively celebrated in other classrooms.

Of course, celebrating success does not ensure that everyone will have great grades and perfect behavior, but it will acknowledge students meeting the classroom goals you have established. Students crave positive attention, which is a powerful motivator. Celebrating student successes can forever change the lives of our students. For many of the students you teach, you could be one of the few positive people in their lives.

Unfortunately, celebrating the success of students is not automatic for every teacher. Putting recognition into practice (and policy) requires zero financial resources. However, what is required is the political will from leadership and other supportive stakeholders to be committed enough to create a culture of recognition" (Rodríguez & Oseguera, 2015). Sadly, there are many classrooms that do not have a positive classroom environment, which results in those students underperforming in all key areas that indicate academic success. These are the classrooms that parents do not want for their children. These are the classrooms that other teachers do not respect. These are the classrooms that principals do not like to visit.

In most classrooms there is much to celebrate. Students are performing well, attendance goals are being met, and students are behaving properly. We need to celebrate these successes daily. Obstacles to regular success may include focusing on misbehaving students and forgetting the many positive student responses of the day. But even in a positive situation, it is possible that students are not being celebrated. I believe there are two possible reasons for this. The first is that the teacher can easily get caught up in managing the few students who behave negatively and forget the many positive choices taking place every day.

The second cause is the Ms. Carltons of the world-teachers who refuse to celebrate the success of students. They see no need to celebrate what is expected. I know that some teachers believe that celebrating success is not important or not part of their job requirement. I wonder how those teachers keep their students motivated. Lowe (2010) suggests the following: share a vision, your school should be a change agent, analyze data, introduce students to their data, and increase rigor. Each of these areas can kick start your efforts to celebrating students.

Although I know that this is controversial, I believe that sometimes it is necessary to offer specific, tangible rewards to students, teachers and parents. Unfortunately, schools that do not have high levels of parent involvement have increased behavior problems and lower academic achievement (Lewis, Kim, & Bey, 2011). One year my school had historically low turnout for parent-teacher conferences. Several staff suggested that we give away some kind of prize during the next parent-teacher conferences. We held a drawing for two gift cards from Home Depot. To my surprise we had a packed house. I didn't initially agree with this strategy, but it worked. If that is what we needed to do to get parents to conferences, we had to do it.

Mr. Rivers is a **SUPERHERO EDUCATOR** that liked to think outside the box. As the principal, he recognized his school was not celebrating student successes like it should. His school had an honor roll, but the same students made it on the list every marking period. Mr. Rivers knew too many students never received recognition and felt something needed to be done to reach all those unrecognized students. If he could reach those students, he hoped, their grades and the school environment would improve.

Mr. Rivers came up with the idea of having a two-step system for celebrating student successes. Step one was to have a student from each classroom recognized every week for outstanding effort, one student for outstanding school behavior, and one student for outstanding improvement—with a conscious focus on honoring students who were rarely acknowledged positively. Step two required the teachers to make a positive phone call to the parents of each of the three students selected that week. Mr. Rivers felt this strategy would better recognize students and that the positive phone calls would improve parent-teacher relationships. When implemented correctly, each classroom teacher would make twelve positive phone calls each month. As a school they set a goal of over two thousand positive phone calls.

To his surprise, not everyone liked Mr. River's plan. The biggest complaint was how much time was needed to make three positive phone calls each week. This was strange, in light of the fact that most of the teachers complaining were daily making many negative phone calls each day. Developing strong parent-teacher partnerships was obviously, and disappointingly, not a high priority at his school, though these relationships have been repeatedly shown to have great potential for student academic and behavioral improvements.

Another complaint pertained to the required documentation of the phone calls on a weekly checklist. This was perceived as micromanaging but was the only way to ensure that the positive phone calls were being made.

In spite of these reservations, the strategy was implemented and the new student recognition and positive phone calls had immediate results, dramatically changing the school environment for the better. The students knew exactly what needed to be done to meet teacher expectations and tried much harder to be successful in school. The process had a particularly positive impact on the students who had never before been celebrated. The under-recognized were now being recognized to their great benefit.

The most profound success of this effort was a dramatic improvement of the school's relationship with the parents. In the past, most parents assumed a phone call from the school meant something negative. Parent after parent indicated that they had never received a positive phone call before for their child. The concept that a phone call could be something positive was an eye opener for both parents and teachers.

SUPERHERO EDUCATORS will always find ways to celebrate the success of their students.

Debriefing Questions

1. What successes do you celebrate in your classroom?

2. Why do you celebrate the success of your students?

3. Research local companies. List two companies that excel in celebrating the success of their employees. Give an example of how they do that.

4. List ten ways in which you can celebrate student success.

5. Reflect on Chapter 14 Visual: How does this image compare to the way your school celebrates success?

6. Observe five different educators. Record and evaluate how each teacher recognizes success.

7. Is there a connection between educators who are not effective and their lack of celebrating students? Evaluate.

8. Reflect on your individual gifts. How can these strengths be used to further celebrate student success?

9. Explain why an educator might not find a reason to celebrate student successes.

10. Explain how stellar celebration of student success can lead to remarkable student achievement.

Notes of Emphasis

CHAPTER 15
Leader Legacy

Superhero Connection

With super strength and quick flight, Mighty Mouse saves the day. Extraordinary rescues or continual crisis, Mighty Mouse leads people to safety. Even when faced with insurmountable odds, Mighty Mouse is relentless and never gives up. Mighty Mouse does not let his size be a barrier or an excuse to lose. Regardless of the size of the task, the leadership of **SUPERHERO EDUCATORS** *is always here to save the day.*

Impact Story

According to Gift Card Granny, gift cards have been the most requested gift nine years running, with about 60% of people in 2015 saying they hoped or expected to receive one ("Gift Card Statistics", 2017). Although Target and McDonald's lead the list of the most popular gift cards (Shin, 2016), my favorite one is for Panera Bread. The last time I used the card it could not be read because of extensive use—the numbers had become unrecognizable and the magnetic strip would not register. The worker asked if I was able to pay in any other manner. I said I could use my credit card, but I'd rather use the gift card. Without hesitation, the worker took the lead, said that my meal was free and provided instructions on how to get a replacement card. I greatly appreciated the problem solving—being empowered to make decisions and solve problems on the spot is essential for any organization of excellence.

You are probably aware of an incident in 2017 during which a customer was very roughly removed from a United Airlines aircraft. The incident was recorded by several passengers on their smart phones and immediately went viral. The public quickly became outraged, United stock fell 250 million dollars and many even demanded the resignation of the president of United.

As a result of this incident United Airlines implemented several changes to their operation to avoid something like this from reoccurring. Employees were empowered to solve such problems on the spot, and United even developed an app that would allow employees to handle customer issues and compensate customers without company authorization. United employees now have permission to act on their own to resolve problems just as the person at Panera had resolved mine.

Innovative Connections

My teenage son got in a very minor car accident. The car ahead of him abruptly stopped. My son slammed on his brakes but still ended up hitting the back bumper of the car. The damage consisted of some scratches and paint removal on the back bumper of the car my son hit. I quickly called our insurance company, Amica, one of the top rated companies in the nation for customer satisfaction ("Top Car Insurance Companies", 2015). The Amica representative gathered the facts quickly and told me they would handle everything. The next day Amica called with a list of items they were handling and within a week everything had been resolved—including the repairs. Amica proved its value to us as its customer. Every aspect was handled efficiently and professionally with no excuses. This is leadership—taking control of the situation and executing solutions.

Educational Research and Focus

SUPERHERO EDUCATORS are leaders. Although we tend to look at the principal or superintendent as the school leader, teachers are also exercising leadership in schools by holding fast to a vision of democratic learning communities and taking actions, small and large, to disrupt inequality and to create real opportunities for students, families, colleagues, and community members (Collay, 2013).

Our current system often limits the impact of teachers by seeing leadership as residing only in formal leadership positions. Teachers see leaving the classroom to take one of those positions as the only way to have influence. From this viewpoint, teachers are leaving their strengths as a classroom teacher behind and being promoted to a position that does not allow them to use their true gifts. And the school has lost a great teacher.

An alternative to this approach is to keep great teachers in their classrooms while providing them with opportunities to exercise informal leadership. In so doing, these teachers would be released from some of the more burdensome duties of teaching and would be rewarded by increased financial compensation.

Great teachers reach their greatest potential in the classroom. Being an expert in a content area or educational theme is crucial to leadership. Students will achieve more when being taught by knowledgeable teachers who are passionate about their content. Parents trust these expert teachers. Staff and faculty members learn from teachers through professional development sessions. Adapting classrooms to meet student needs by going above and beyond in preparation for instructional delivery develops true believers.

In a faculty meeting, for example, a principal emphasizes that she wants everyone to start his or her classes on time and get in as many quality instructional minutes as possible. She sympathizes with the faculty, knowing that drills, parent meetings, and immediate student concerns may delay the start of class. Adam, an 8th grade teacher, raises his hand and announces to all present that he never starts his classes late. He continues by discussing how unprofessional it is to start class late. These actions by Adam are not leadership, but rather highlighting his own achievements.

Genuine teacher leadership takes the principal's request, believes it is in the best interest of students, and works diligently to ensure all instructional minutes are held. When this happens, others notice and will inquire about his or her teaching skills and instructional habits. Teaching is a messy business, requiring us to be theoretically grounded and purposeful while we respond to the many daily challenges (Gergen, 2009).

Accountability is another trademark of strong leadership. During one of my first years as a principal, I had a first year teacher who truly loved his students and wanted the best for each one of them. Unfortunately, in one incident, he penalized a student for not turning in his homework assignment when in fact the student had—the teacher had simply mislaid it. The student's dad heard that his son was penalized because the teacher was unable to find the assignment and quickly came to the school to display his frustration to the teacher. After listening to the parent rant about his teaching ineffectiveness, the teacher calmly apologized to the parent. The whole situation was resolved quickly. The teacher accepted accountability for the problem without hesitation—no excuses, no confusing teacher language, and no casting blame on the student. This refreshing approach by the teacher calmed the situation, and, more importantly, gained the respect of both student and parent.

Pointing fingers and complaining about students does little to establish a culture of respect. Taking accountability is not always easy, but honest accountability builds lasting influence. Having followers that support teachers in the challenges of moving an organization into uncharted and often highly risky territory is lasting influence (Branson, 2014).

Anticipation is a leadership skill that can be and must be developed. Anticipate what will come to you as a teacher every day, so you will be prepared and be able to meet these challenges. Not all students will be done with their homework. Some students will talk when you are talking. Other students will not participate or engage in the lesson. Students will get up out of their seats. Parents will email you late at night and early in the morning asking lengthy questions. Your administrator will ask you to do something unexpected in your classroom. Co-workers will disappoint you. What are you going to do when these predictable situations happen? Plan out your action steps. Anticipate what you will do before they happen and avoid negative teacher outcomes. Teacher leaders anticipate what will happen in their classrooms and creatively problem solve.

SUPERHERO EDUCATORS vigorously seek feedback. When lessons are delivered and instruction is given, teachers want honest feedback. Traditionally, schools dispense feedback as part of a supervision of instruction program. The school principal meets with the teacher for a pre-conference, observes the teacher, and then conducts a post-conference. This whole process is usually conducted twice a year. Innovation has swept into some school districts and now administrators are implementing walk-throughs. Walk-throughs are informal visits by administrators highlighting a targeted area such as questioning or formative assessments. The benefit of walk-throughs is that the frequency of visits and feedback can increase dramatically. Leaders want to know where they stand today and how they can improve. And they definitely want to become the best teachers they can be!

Leadership is not a license to do less; it is a responsibility to do more. And that's the trouble. Leadership takes work. It takes time and energy. The effects are not always easily measured and they are not always immediate. Leadership is always a commitment to human beings (Sinek, 2014). Teacher leaders are **SUPERHERO EDUCATORS**.

Debriefing Questions

1. Cite an occasion when you observed a business display bold leadership from its workers.

2. Define "teacher leader".

3. How do we improve our educational system so teachers can stay in the classroom and still execute leadership responsibilities?

4. Are there times when you cannot or should not be honest with your principal or parents?

5. Reflect on Chapter 15 Visual: Predict your largest obstacle to becoming a teacher leader.

6. How do you handle positive feedback?

7. If you struggle to anticipate and see what is "around the corner", what can you do as an educator to improve in this area?

8. Why do you want to be a teacher leader?

9. How do you become a teacher leader?

10. What is your approach, as a leader, to handling conflict?

Notes of Emphasis

CONCLUSION

What did you make with Legos when you were a child? Stretching your imagination, Legos provides new freedoms and joy in creation. Vividly, I remember creatively building with Legos in my family's basement for hours and hours. Legos was founded in 1932, became a household name, and today is one of the largest manufacturer of toys. The name 'LEGO' is an abbreviation of two Danish words "leg godt", meaning "play well". The name defines Legos; it represents the ideal (Mortensen, 2015). In downtown Chicago, Illinois, there is a Lego store that attracts thousands of visitors because of its vibrancy and imagination. Young children are captivated by an enormous Lego Star Wars Stormtrooper, while adults are mystified by the Chicago skyline made out of Legos. Money flows freely as this experience of visiting a big toy store is enjoyed.

Years of research on teacher quality supports the fact that effective teachers not only cultivate students' feelings about school and learning, but also that their work actually results in increased student achievement. The idea of superheroes flourish in movies and merchandise. People yearn to have hope, a reason to dream. Positive energy and confidence fill the mind when a superhero takes action and brings order to the chaos. Superheroes restore justice and achieve results. They are not perfect, but they always improve the situation. That is why educators can so easily be compared with superheroes. Teachers must use their many talents to bring hope, high expectations, and positive results to today's students. Teaching with superior skills and success is a process that requires hard work, dedication, and continual learning. The content in this book provides the framework for any teacher to become a **SUPERHERO EDUCATOR**. These heroes create a better world for us all, one student at a time (Florence, 2010).

You are a **SUPERHERO EDUCATOR!**

Utilizing the book's chapter titles, draw yourself as a superhero. Include your top three strengths as superhero tools. Also, identify your biggest area of improvement (your kryptonite) in your drawing.

REFERENCES

A new vision of excellence in assessment. (2017). Retrieved from http://rickstiggins.com/

Ahmad, N., Walter, H., & Sherman, H. (2016). The home away from home: An analysis of the lodging industry in 2015. *American Journal of Entrepreneurship*, 9(1), 60-81.

Alexander, A. (2017). Apple's mission statement. Retrieved from https://alvinalexander.com/blog/post/mac-os-x/apple-business-philosophy-mission-statement

Allen, K. (2012). *Amazon.com tops in customer service, according to NRF foundation/american express survey.* Retrieved from according-nrf-foundationamerican-express-survey

Anderson, D. & Anderson, J. (2010). *Report cards to paychecks: get fired up strategies for succeeding in college and in life.* United States of America: DWA Holdings.

Archer, D. (2015). 3 *customer-centric lessons from Amazon.* Retrieved from https://www.myfeelback.com/en/blog/customer-centric-lessons-amazon

Armstrong, P. (2017). *Bloom's taxonomy.* Retrieved https://cft.vanderbilt.edufrom/guides-sub-pages/blooms-taxonomy/

As diversity increases, will U.S. be more or less politically divided? (2017). Retrieved from http://www.pbs.org/newshour/bb/diversity-increases-will-u-s-less-politically-divided/

Avitabile, J. (2007). Teachers offer tips on organization skills: I have to get organized. *School Planning & Mangagement*, 46(2), 40-44, 46.

Bailey, S. (2015). Best Buy: The largest consumer electronics retailer. Retrieved from http://marketrealist.com/2015/01/best-buy-largest-consumer-electronics-retailer/

Benefits of data warehouses for business. (2015). Retrieved from http://www.techadvisory.org/2015/03/benefits-of-data-warehouses-for-business/

Bloomberg-Company Overview of Uber Technologies. (2017). Retrieved from https://www.bloomberg.com/research/stocks/private/snapshot.asp?privcapId=144524848

Bluestein, J. (2012). Build flexibility into your homework schedule. Retrieved from http://www.educationworld.com/a_curr/bluestein-homework-policies-flexibility.shtml

Boon, H. J., Brown, L. H., Tsey, K., Speare, R., Pagliano, P., Usher, K., & Clark, B. (2011). School disaster planning for children with disabilities: A critical review of the literature. *International Journal of Special Education*, 26, 1-14.

Branson, R. (2014). *The virgin way.* New York: Penguin Group.

Carson, B. (2015). Mark Zuckerberg says he's giving away 99% of his Facebook shares—worth $45 billion today. Retrieved from http://www.businessinsider.com/mark-zuckerberg-giving-away-99-of-his-facebook-shares-2015-12

Ceccherini, S. (2016). The do's and don'ts of employee wellness programs. *Business NH Magazine, 33*(9), 47-48. Retrieved from http://searchproquest.com.cuw.ezproxy.switchinc.org/docview/1824190263?accountid=10249

Christensen Institute-Disruptive Innovation. (2017). Retrieved from https://www.christenseninstitute.org/key-concepts/disruptive-innovation-2/

Claxton, G., Rae, M., Pancha, N., Whitmore, H., Damico, A., Kenward, K., & Long, M. (2015). Health benefits in 2015: Stable trends in the employer market. *Health Affairs, 34*(10), 1779-1788.

Cleland, B., McKay, C., Danielson, C., & Axtell, D. (2009). *Implementing the framework for teaching in enhancing professional practice.* Alexandria, VA: Association for Supervision and Curriculum Development.

Collay, M. (2013). *Teaching is leading.* Alexandria, VA: Association for Supervision and Curriculum Development.

Consumer reports-about us. (2017). Retrieved from http://www.con-sumerreports.org/cro/about-us/index.htm

Cox, J. (2016). Dealing with cleanliness in the classroom. Retrieved from https://www.thoughtco.com/dealing-with-cleanliness-in-the-classroom-2081581

Dabbs, L. (2012). New-teacher academy: Lesson planning. Retrieved from https://www.edutopia.org/blog/new-teacher-lesson-planning-lisa-dabbs

Davis, S, V. (2014). Kohl's new wellness center aims to attract top talent. Retrieved from https://www.bizjournals.com/milwaukee from/blog/2014/06/kohls-new-wellness-center-aims-to-attract-top.html

Desilver, D. (2017). U.S. students' academic achievement still lags that of their peers in many other countries. Retrieved from http://www.pewresearch.org/fact-tank/2017/02/15/u-s-students-internationally-math-science/

Digest of Education Statistics. (2015). Retrieved from https://nces.ed.gov/programs/digest/d15/

Disis, J. (2016). Black Friday 2016: More shoppers, less spending. Retrieved from http://money.cnn.com/2016/11/27/news/companies/black-friday-national-retail-federation/index.html

Drapeau, P. (2014). *Student creativity: Practical ways to promote innovative thinking and problem solving.* Alexandria, VA: Association for Supervision and Curriculum Development.

Duff, V. (2017). Plumbing industry analysis. Retrieved from http://small-business.chron.com/plumbing-industry-analysis-76545.html

Durgin, J. (2016). How to plan for a substitute teacher. Retrieved from http://www.cfclassroom.com/2016/03/how-to-plan-for-a-substitute-teacher.html

Ferrier, L. (2016). Student life–tips for managing stress. *Nursing Standard, 31*(7), 35.

Four types of questions that increase rigor (2015). Retrieved from http://www.marzanocenter.com/blog/article/four-types-of-questions-that-increase-rigor/

Florence, N. (2010). *Multiculturalism 101.* New York: McGraw-Hill.

Gaines, K. (2016). Sleepless in America: Burning the candle at both ends? At what cost? *Urologic Nursing, 36*(3), 109-110.

Gallavan N, (2011). *Navigating cultural competence in grades 6-12: A compass for teachers.* Thousand Oaks, CA: Corwin.

Gates M. (2013). Reclaiming the "art and science" of teaching. Retrieved from http://www.huffingtonpost.com/melinda-gates/reclaiming-the-art-and-sc_b_26635

GE Recognized as one of the top 10 most community-minded companies in America. (2012). Retrieved from http://newsroom.gehealthcare.com/ge-recognized-as-one-of-the-top-10-most-community-minded-companies-in/

Genishi, C., & Dyson, A. H. (2009). *Children, language, and literacy: Diverse Learners in Diverse Times*. New York: Teachers College Press.

Gergen, K. (2009). *Relational being: Beyond self and community*. Oxford, UK: Oxford University Press.

Geving, A. M. (2007). Identifying the types of student and teacher behaviors associated with teacher stress. *Teaching and Teacher Education: An International Journal of Research and Studies, 23*, 624–640.

Gift Card Statistics. (2017). Retrieved from https://www.giftcardgranny.com/statistics/

Goldenberg, B. (2013). White teachers in urban classrooms. *Urban Education. 49*(1), 111-144.

Gollnick, D. & Chinn, P. (2017). *Multicultural education in a pluralistic society*. Boston, MA: Pearson Education.

GoodReads Quotes (2017). Retrieved from https://www.goodreads.com/quotes

Grant, R. (2013). 6 companies that dominate 6 industries thanks to data. Retrieved from https://venturebeat.com/2013/12/04/6-companies-dominating-with-data-across-6-industries/

Hall, P. & Simeral, A. (2015). *Teach, reflect, learn: Building your capacity for success in the classroom*. Alexandria, VA: Association for Supervision and Curriculum Development.

Hanes, T. (2017). Reasons why it is important to eat healthy foods to stay healthy. Retrieved from http://www.livestrong.com/article/82340-reasons-important-eat-foods-stay/

Hargreaves, A., & Fink, D. (2007). *Sustainable Leadership.* San Francisco, CA: Jossey Bass.

How it started (2017). Retrieved from http://www.espnfounder.com/how_it_started.htm

Hyatt, N. (2017). Autonomous driving is here, and it's going to change everything. Retrieved from https://www.recode.net/2017/4/19/15364608 / autonomous-self-driving-cars-impact-disruption-society-mobility

James, G. (2013). 4 keys to customer loyalty. Retrieved from https://www.inc.com/geoffrey-james/4-keys-to-customer-loyalty.html?cid=s

Kafele, B. (2015). The principal 50: Critical leadership questions for inspiring schoolwide excellence. Alexandria, VA: Association for Supervision and Curriculum Development.

Kayler, M., DeMulder, E. K., View, J. L., & Stribling, S. M. (2009). Cultivating transformative leadership in P-12 schools and classrooms through critical teacher professional development. *Journal of Curriculum and Instruction, 3*(2), 39-53.

Kline, P. & Saunders, B. (2010). *Ten Steps to a learning Organization.* Salt Lake City, UT: Great River Books

Knight, P. (2016). *Shoe dog: A memoir of the creator of NIKE.* New York: Simon & Schuster.

Koppelman, K. (2017). *Understanding human differences: Multicultural education for a diverse America.* Boston, MA: Pearson Education.

Kowal, J. & Brinson, D. (2011, April 14). Beyond classroom walls: developing innovative work roles for teachers. Retrieved from https://www.

americanprogress.org/issues/education/reports/2011/04/14/9527/beyond-classroom-walls/

Korzeniowski, P. (2016). How to make your workplace culture collaborative. Retrieved http://www.informationweek from.com/strategic-cio/how-to-make-your-workplace-culture-collaborative/a/d-id/1324704

Lapowsky, I. (2017, January 1). Trump's data firm snags rnc tech guru darren bolding. Retrieved from https://www.wired.com/2017/01/trumps-data-firm-snags-republican-national-committee-cto/

Ladson-Billings, G. (2009). *The dream keepers: Successful teachers of African American children.* San Francisco, CA: Wiley.

Lee, D. (2013). How twitter changed the world, hashtag by hashtag. Retrieved from http://www.bbc.com/news/technology-24802766

Lennon, S. J., Johnson, K., & Lee, J. (2011). A perfect storm for consumer misbehavior: Shopping on Black Friday. *Clothing and Textiles Research Journal, 29*(2), 119-134.

Lewis L. L., Kim Y. A., Bey J. A. (2011). Teaching practices and strategies to involve inner city parents at home and in the school. *Teaching and Teacher Education, 27*(1), 221-234.

Lewis, M. (2017). Is an extended warranty worth the cost?–When to buy or avoid. Retrieved from http://www.moneycrashers.com/extended-warranty-worth-cost/

Linsin, M. (2009). A classroom management strategy every teacher should use. Retrieved from https://www.smartclassroommanagement.com/2009/10/17/a-classroom-management-strategy-every-teacher-should-use/

Linsin, M. (2012). How to end each day on the right classroom management foot. Retrieved from https://www.smartclassroommanagement.com/2012/02/11/how-to-end-each-day-on-the-right-classroom-management-foot/

Losen, D. J. & Gillespie, J. (2012). Opportunities suspended: The disparate impact of disciplinary exclusion from school. Retrieved from: https://www.civilrightsproject.ucla.edu/resources/projects/center-for-civil-rights-remedies/school-to-prison-folder/federal-reports/upcoming-ccrr-research

Louis K. S. & Wahlstrom K. (2011). Principals as cultural leaders. *Phi Delta Kappan*, 92(5), 52-56.

Lowe, P. (2010). Top 10 ways to improve student achievement and create learners. Retrieved from http://www.huffingtonpost.com/pam-lowe/top-10-ways-to-improve-st_b_786205.html

Ma, X., & Crocker, R. (2007). Provincial effects on reading achievement. *Alberta Journal of Educational Research*. 53, 87-108.

Mandelbaum, A. (2015, October 29). Hotel technology innovations that will drive business in 2016. Retrieved from: https://www.hospitalitynet.org/opinion/4072364.html

Marques, F. (2014). People and purpose: what Amazon's Jeff Bezos teaches us about values. Retrieved from http://www.ims.gs/blog/people-purpose-amazons-jeff-bezos-teaches-us-values/

Marzano, R. (2011). *Formative assessment and standardized-based grading*. Bloomington, IN: Solution Tree Press.

Miltenberger, R. G. (2008). *Behavior modification: Principles and procedures* (4th ed.). Belmont, CA: Brooks/Cole.

Milner, IV, H.R. (2010). *Start where you are, but don't stay there: Understanding diversity, opportunity gaps, and teaching in today's classrooms.* Cambridge, MA: Harvard Educational Press.

Minkle, K. M., Sheridan, S. M., Kim, E.M., Ryoo, J.H., & Koziol, N. A. (2014). Congruence in parent-teacher relationships. *Elementary School Journal, 114*(4), 527-546.

Mission statement of UPS (2013). Retrieved from https://www.strategicman-agementinsight.com/mission-statements/ups-mission-statement.html

Moral Compassing. (2009). Retrieved from http://www.franklincovey.ca/FCCAWeb/aspx/library_articles_gen5.htm

Mortensen, T.F. (2015). The LEGO group history. Retrieved from https://www.lego.com/en-us/aboutus/lego-group/the_lego_history

Nethers, D. (2014). Vegan teacher fired over Facebook post. Retrieved from http://fox8.com/2014/12/12/vegan-teacher-fired-over-facebook-post/

Numbers of mobile phone users worldwide from 2013 2019. (2017). Retrieved from https://www.statista.com/statistics/274774/forecast-of-mobile-phone-users-worldwide/

Olavsrud, T. (2017). 15 data and analytics trends that will dominate 2017. Retrieved from http://www.cio.com/article/3166060/analytics/15-data-and-analytics-trends-that-will-dominate-2017.html

Otenyo, E. E., & Smith, E. A. (2017). An overview of employee wellness pro-grams (EWPs) in large U.S. cities. *Public Personnel Management, 46*(1), 3-24.

Palmer D. (2007). What is the best way to motivate students in science? *Teaching Science: The Journal of the Australian Science Teachers Association, 53*(1), 38-42.

Paredes, M. (2010). Academic parent-teacher teams: reorganizing parent- teacher conferences around data. Retrieved from http://www.hfrp. org/publications-resources/browse-our-publications/academic-parent-teacher-teams-reorganizing-parent-teacher-conferences-around-data

Pitcher, S. M., Albright, L. K., DeLaney, C. J., Walker, N. T., Deonarinesingh, K., & Mogge, S. (2007). Assessing adolescents' motivation to read. *Journal of Adolescent & Adult Literacy. 50*(5), 378–396.

Puentedura, R. (2014). SAMR and bloom's taxonomy: assembling the puzzle. Retrieved https://www.commonsense.org/fromeducation/blog/samr-and-blooms-taxonomy-assembling-the-puzzle

Rathel, J., Drasgow, E., Brown, W. H., Marshall, K. J. (2013). Increasing induction-level teachers' positive-to-negative communication ratio and use of behavior-specific praise through e-mailed performance feedback and its effect on students' task engagement. *Journal of Positive Behavior Interventions, 16*(4), 219-233.

Rhomberg, A. (2015). In god we trust, all others must bring data. Retrieved from http://www.digitalbookworld.com/2015/in-god-we-trust-all-others-must-bring-data/

Ripples-Make a ripple on the world. (2017). Retrieved from http://www.coffeeripples.com/https:/sso.cuw.edu/cas/logout?url=http%3A%2F%2Fmy.cuw.edu&sessionLogoutComplete=true

Rodríguez, L, F. & Oseguera, L. (2015). Our deliberate success. *Journal of Hispanic Higher Education. 14*(2), 128-150.

Rollins, S. (2017) *Teaching in the fast lane: How to create active learning experiences.* Alexandria, VA: Association for Supervision and Curriculum Development.

Roorda, D. L., Koomen, H. Y. K., Split, J. L., & Oort, F. J. (2011). The influence of affective teacher-student relationships on students' school engagement and achievement. *Review of Educational Research, 81*(4), 493–529.

Rose, M. & Blodgett, J. (2016). Should hotels respond to negative online reviews. *Cornell Hospitality Quarterly, 57*(4), 396-410.

Sanborn, M. (2008). *How to provide extraordinary customer service: The Fred factor.* [Video File]. Retrieved from https://www.youtube.com/watch?v=4GKQ9kTnSg4

Satell, G. (2014). A look back at why blockbuster really failed and why it didn't. Retrieved from https://www.forbes.com/sites/gregsatell/2014/09/05/a-look-back-at-why-blockbuster-really-failed-and-why-it-didnt-have-to/#406568271d64

Shah, S. (2017). 10 most ethical companies in US. Retrieved from http://www.insidermonkey.com/blog/10-most-ethical-companies-in-the-us-533013/

Shin, L. (2016). The best gift cards to give in 2016. Retrieved from https://www.forbes.com/sites/laurashin/2016/11/30/the-best-gift-cards-to-give-in-2016/#607b49f0640d

Sinek, S. (2014). *Leaders eat last: Why some teams pull together and others don't.* New York: Penguin Books.

Smallen, D. (2016). 2015 U.S.-based airline traffic data. Retrieved from https://www.rita.dot.gov/bts/press_releases/bts018_16

Southan, J. (2016). Missing in action. *Business Traveler (Asia-Pacific Edition),* 36-39.

Souto-Manning, M., & Martell, J. (2017). Committing to culturally relevant literacy teaching as an everyday practice: It's critical! *Language Arts*, 94(4), 252-256.

Stronge, J. (2012). *Qualities of effective teachers.* Alexandria, VA: Association for Supervision and Curriculum Development.

Study: NBA diversity again leads pro sports leagues. (2014). Retrieved from https://www.usatoday.com/story/sports/nba/2015/07/01/study-nba-diversity-again-leads-pro-sports-leagues/29577091/

Teacher evaluation-the marzano teacher evaluation model. (2017). Retrieved from http://www.marzanocenter.com/Teacher-Evaluation/

The Framework. (2017). Retrieved from http://www.danielsongroup.org / framework/

Thompson, D. (2013). The global dominance of ESPN: Why hasn't anybody figured out how to beat "The Worldwide Leader in Sports"? Retrieved from https://www.theatlantic.com/magazine/archive/2013/09/the-most-valuable-network/309433/

Top car insurance companies that won't break the budget. (2015). Retrieved from https://www.consumerreports.org/cro/news/2015/08/top-car-insurance-companies-that-wont-break-the-budget/index.htm

Trimble, M. (2017). Harvard pulls admission offers after explicit posts. Retrieved from https://www.usnews.com/news/national-news/articles/2017-06-05/harvard-pulls-student-admission-offers-after-explicit-facebook-posts

Verbal ping pong: Learn to love your elevator speech. (2017). Retrieved from https://www.extrememeetings.com/speaking-programs/verbal-ping-pong/

Vision 2020 (2017). Retrieved from http://www.samsung.com/uk/aboutsamsung/

Wazwaz, N. (2015). It's Official: The U.S. is becoming a minority-majority nation. Retrieved from https://www.usnews.com/news/articles/2015/07/06/its-official-the-us-is-becoming-a-minority-majority-nation

Wells, A. S., Fox, L., & Cordova-Cobo, D. (2016). How racially diverse schools and classrooms can benefit all students. *The Education Digest, 82*(1), 17-24.

What is cloud computing? (2017). Retrieved from https://www.salesforce.com/cloudcomputing/

Who We Are (2017). Retrieved from http://solutions.3m.com/wps/portal/3M/en_US/3M-Company/Information/AboutUs/WhoWeAre/

Workplace motivation goes beyond the paycheck. (2015, October 5). Retrieved from https://www.vocoli.com/blog/october-2015/workplace-motivation-goes-beyond-the-paycheck/

White, S. H. (2009). *Leadership maps.* Englewood, CO: Lead & Learn Press.

WIggins, G. (2012). Seven keys of effective feedback. *Educational Leadership, 70*(1),10-15.

Wolfe, P. (2010). *Brain matters: Translating research into classroom practice.* (2nd ed.) Alexandria, VA: Association for Supervision and Curriculum Development.

World's best cat litter. (2017) Retrieved from https://www.worldsbestcatlitter.com/our-difference/

Zeilinger, J. (2013). 7 reasons why risk-taking leads to success. Retrieved from http://www.huffingtonpost.com/2013/08/13/seven-reasons-why-risk-taking-leads-to-success_n_3749425.html